Turning a School Around

Turning a School Around

Key Considerations for Real Success

Josh Martin

ROWMAN & LITTLEFIELD
Lanham • Boulder • New York • London

Published by Rowman & Littlefield
An imprint of The Rowman & Littlefield Publishing Group, Inc.
4501 Forbes Boulevard, Suite 200, Lanham, Maryland 20706
www.rowman.com

6 Tinworth Street, London SE11 5AL

Copyright © 2020 by Josh Martin

All rights reserved. No part of this book may be reproduced in any form or by any electronic or mechanical means, including information storage and retrieval systems, without written permission from the publisher, except by a reviewer who may quote passages in a review.

British Library Cataloguing in Publication Information Available

Library of Congress Control Number: 2019950642
ISBN 9781475853285 (cloth : alk. paper)
ISBN 9781475853292 (pbk. : alk. paper)
ISBN 9781475853308 (electronic)

To my wife, Amber, who has always believed in me at a level only she can, and to my daughters, Aubrey and Hailey, who I hope always have teachers in their lives who love what they do and are able to provide the amazing learning opportunities they deserve.

Contents

Preface ix

Introduction xi

1 Yes, the Teacher Matters, but So Does the Principal 1

2 Instruction—What's the Difference between Talking the Talk and Walking the Walk? 23

3 Formative Assessment: The Truest Evaluator of Quality When Evaluating Lessons 43

4 Are You Making Time to Get into Classrooms or Excuses That Keep You Out? 67

5 Become a Data Storyteller 85

About the Author 103

Preface

The motivation in writing this book comes from the need to stress the pivotal role of the principal on the outcomes of students in the classroom. In my time as a teacher, principal, and central office administrator, I have witnessed firsthand the positive and negative impact of principals on a campus through their ability to execute their role as instructional leader.

With such an emphasis on school turnaround in our profession, as educators we must ask ourselves, "How do we achieve the real change necessary to turn around our schools?" People see this as an opportunity to market curriculum, test banks, and a whole host of schemes to solve the needs of struggling schools. The reason many of these options fail is that they do not address the root cause: campus leadership.

This can be demonstrated through my own personal experience. I once thought a campus would be fine with strong teachers in spite of poor instructional leadership by the principal, and I was surprised by poor results. On the other side of the coin, I found myself equally surprised by a campus with strong instructional leadership from a principal who was able to achieve more than I thought she could, despite having marginal teachers. Through these experiences, I have realized that the possibilities are endless for campuses where a strong instructional leader can lead and grow a staff of strong teachers.

At the end of the day, there is much professional development and literature that discuss the impact of the teacher on student achievement and many buzzwords and acronyms dealing with increasing student achievement. Ultimately, we must realize the important impact of the principal. All great organizations require great leaders, and settling for anything less is failing our teachers and students.

Introduction

This book examines the responsibilities of the principal in creating instructional change. It can be argued that there is no more important position on the campus than that of the principal—not because the principal is a disciplinarian or supervisor but because he is an instructional leader. It is in this role that the principal determines the success of a campus. A principal who falls short as an instructional leader can be more detrimental than poor teachers are to the classroom.

In order to determine what is required to effectively live up to the role of principal, this book explores the difference between talking the talk and walking the walk in a profession driven by flashy jargon and a complicated web of acronyms. To create real change, the change required in turning around low-performing schools, you must be able to navigate through the nonsense and identify principals who know and understand instruction.

The other key to being able to turn around campuses is effectively using formative assessment. What this instructional tool lacks in flash it makes up in effectiveness for instructional leaders. Formative assessment put to proper use provides invaluable feedback to teachers not only about student understanding but also on the effectiveness of teachers' lessons.

This book also examines the essential requirement that principals are in classrooms. Why should principals be in classrooms? And why it is so important to not to allow excuses to keep them out? The mantra of chapter 4 is "Inspect what you expect." If principals make grandiose plans for instruction without following up to make sure they are being implemented, chances are they will not be.

Finally, it is important for principals to know their data. I delineate the difference between surface knowledge of data and really digging in to allow the data to tell students' stories. If principals can read the story the data is telling, they will find it exponentially easier to understand what to do for their teachers and students.

Chapter One

Yes, the Teacher Matters, but So Does the Principal

You know how children talk about what they want to be when they grow up? Doctors, firefighters, and astronauts come to mind initially. They also want to be teachers. You want to know a job that rarely, if ever, ends up on the list? Principal. Why are two jobs within the same profession seen so differently?

The first step in answering that question is to look at how each position is viewed. Teaching is seen as an inspiring and rewarding profession—a career where teachers leave a legacy of sorts with their students while molding the lives of those who will shape the future. How is the principal viewed? Most people would view the principal as the mean guy who hands out the discipline. The dreaded principal's office carries a connotation of fear and despair, arguably for both students and teachers alike.

If you want to set off a wildfire of debate, ask educators which position is more crucial. You will never hear an educator disagree that the teacher in the classroom matters. There is copious research supporting the case. Some of the most influential researchers in the education field have provided stockpiles of data to prove that the teacher is the number one factor in student achievement. If you agree with the research and accept that the teacher in the classroom is the most important factor in student achievement, then what level of importance should we place on campus principals? To find that answer, ask yourself the following questions:

- Who is responsible for hiring those teachers?

- Who is responsible for evaluating the effectiveness of those teachers?
- Who has the unenviable responsibility of removing teachers when they are ineffective?

Some questions get lost in discussions about the duties of a campus principal. Ensuring that a quality teacher is providing quality instruction in every classroom is arguably the most important responsibility of a principal. This responsibility, however, is often the responsibility we think of least.

Sometimes it is difficult for principals to prioritize this crucial responsibility because of the many hats they have to wear as administrators. Because this book spends a lot of time asking more of principals, it is important I first delineate all the duties a principal must perform. In addition to everything that is asked of the principal, these responsibilities do not go away or get exchanged for what this book suggests for principals. A principal's many roles include:

- facilities manager
- disciplinarian
- supervisor
- mentor
- teacher
- instructional leader
- change agent

First up is the principal's role as facilities manager. A generation ago, people viewed this as one of the principal's most important roles. In this role, a principal is responsible for the maintenance and upkeep of the school building, parking lots, and school grounds. If there is a problem with the lights, the plumbing, the kitchen, or anything else on a school property, the principal is charged with getting it fixed.

People come to school principals expecting these issues to be a top priority. These, after all, are issues that directly affect staff, the issues that alter their personal universe. Although important and at times urgent, these responsibilities leave the principal wondering what in the world all of her education was for.

In all seriousness, there is a heavy burden with this hat, as it truly does entail a great deal. Think about logistics alone. One cannot run a school without a master schedule, a bell schedule, a lunch schedule, or a bus schedule. Much can be said of a campus through these various schedules, especially when one considers the master schedule and, to a lesser extent, the bell schedule. Is the principal making every effort to maximize instructional time and opportunity, or is the principal simply plodding through this task, making sure every student has a place to be each period throughout the day?

In addition, consider the time spent during standardized-testing season. Coordinating testing efforts requires creating testing groups, setting up rooms, and securely preparing testing materials, to be returned when finished. Tallying the numerous hours spent on testing season alone shows that principals must use their time and resources well. If a principal has assistants, tasks can be delegated. If not, principals should make sure the rigors of testing season do not take time away from their role as instructional leaders of teachers and students. Many of the tasks during standardized-testing season can be done when everyone else is gone.

In addition, throughout the school year, the principal coordinates all the day-to-day logistics issues. The principal must organize field trips, open houses, dances, and a host of other events. Principals also have required meetings for special programs, such as special education and 504 programs. Principals have all of this to do, and that does not include impromptu meetings with teachers, parents, and others. Are you ready to discuss the other six hats principals are required to wear?

Disciplinarian is the role most people outside of education believe defines principals. It is also the role principals tend to like the least. At the end of the day, there is no way to avoid discipline being part of the job for principals. It would be nice, however, if principals were seen more as developers and implementers of a discipline management plan than as the mean and scary gatekeepers of detention.

What many outsiders and students do not understand is that the whole point of a discipline management plan is to change behavior, not just to dole out consequences. Unfortunately, students view principals as a disciplinarian. However, to get the full effect of this role of disciplinarian, relating to parents during discipline matters needs to be addressed.

For parents, the most dreaded phone number to pop up on their caller IDs is the principal's. Ever notice how surprised parents are when educators call and have something good to say? Seriously though, think how much time principals spend handling student discipline with parents. Parents typically fall into two groups: those who support the school's position and those who defend the student.

Usually the school-supporting group requires the least time. They want the facts and will deal with the rest at home. The student-defending group is usually much more time-consuming. All too often, this group spends an inordinate amount of time declaring their child's innocence, despite all the evidence to the contrary. In addition, the defensive group often wants to negotiate discipline, usually in the form of lessening the consequences. Despite being a hat principals prefer not to wear, student discipline will always be a part of the narrative for principals because the buck has to stop somewhere.

As scary as they are to the students as the disciplinarian, principals, in their supervisory role, are equally scary to teachers. From a teacher's perspective, principals have the power to wreck entire days with random observations (by being the heartless, judging evaluator who has forgotten what it is like to be in the classroom) and the stress these visits cause for teachers.

Principals are in charge of making people get to work too early, and they are the ones who hold them too late in the evenings. Teachers often have to fill out ridiculous amounts of paperwork because of the principal and attend staff meetings to hear from the principal. Principals who define themselves through the role of supervisor are often the reason for the negative connotations of the profession.

Like the previously discussed principal hats, the supervisor hat is a necessary evil. Someone in every organization has to be responsible for making and enforcing the rules. There are ways to accomplish this without being the supervillain, though. Essentially, to truly lead, a principal has to be someone worth following. Part of that involves respecting the staff, their time, their input, and as people in general. A principal can accomplish a lot through conviction, compassion, and effective communication.

As unpleasant as the first few hats can be at times, there are reasons people are excited to become principals. A role that principals feel is a duty and tend to enjoy is that of mentor. Whether for the students or the staff, principals have a good feeling at the end of the day knowing they have made a positive impact on people's lives.

For instance, principals may have a student who turns a corner and makes better choices. Also, principals may have teachers who want to be mentored and guided into a principalship of their own. Just as educators can name the teacher who first drew them to teaching, there is likely a principal who drew you into administration.

Principals should make sure they are dedicating much effort to this role of mentor. As principals, it is incredibly important to make time for students in need, especially those who spend most of their time in the principal's office for other reasons. Principals should also not forget their mentoring responsibility to their teachers. Our profession will never have enough quality teachers. Therefore, the more master teachers we can get to sit in principals' chairs and to lead campuses, the better off our profession will be.

The last three roles are undervalued by most but are definitely some of the most important roles of the principal. The role of teacher is one we do not normally think of when we think of principals. Yet the principal should ultimately be hired to fill the role of master teacher for a school. As discussed throughout this book, principals need to be able to address every instructional need of teachers, both perceived and not. The principal should be able to address instructional issues and also must be respected enough in instructional matters to be viewed as a trusted advisor.

Another hat the principal must wear is that of a change agent. This hat is one of the heavier ones. Change is tough, and it can be extremely so with a large staff of adults. Principals must be able to identify the changes needed to implement change effectively and know how to follow through successfully to ensure sustainability. Principals then must garner buy-in among their staff. Being unsuccessful in implementing change initiatives can put chinks in a principal's leadership armor.

As you will hear over and over, communication is paramount. When solving problems or encouraging change, it is important to collaborate with those involved, not only to hear all perspectives, but also to communicate your point of view and rationale. The ultimate goal is resolution, but sometimes winning, for both sides, entails a mutual understanding. In other words, people can disagree on the final resolution, as long as all involved parties fully understand why the selected direction was chosen. Of course, ideally, collaborations end with everyone agreeing with the resolution. However, that is not always the case.

Finally, the main focus of this book is the principal's role as the instructional leader. Someone must be responsible for the instructional program of the campus, from creation to implementation. If a campus or district hires a principal who cannot carry out this principal's role, the school is almost assuredly doomed to fail. The danger with failing to meet this requirement is that it is not only the principal who fails but also the teachers and students.

Indeed, the wrong person in this critical position can lead to a total campus failure.

The hats of facilities manager, disciplinarian, and supervisor are all important to the daily operation of a campus but logistical in nature. Logistical items take up chunks of time and present themselves as priorities. That is because they are usually in-the-moment tasks and typically something principals can check off a list. Building a staff of highly effective teachers while wearing the hats of a mentor, teacher, change agent, and instructional leader is not something one can check off at the end of the day. These responsibilities are part of ongoing processes that require the highest priority.

What do we mean specifically by *instructional program*, and how does one go about implementing an instructional program? First and foremost, establishing an instructional program is about finding which practices are the most important in maximizing student achievement on the principal's campus. Preferably, principals should rely on data-driven practices that are proven to increase student achievement. The tricky part is that no two campuses are the same, and given that, one plan may not work on every campus.

The key is to understand which practices will be most beneficial for the students on a campus. Principals do not need to randomly select from an instructional grab bag, nor should they try to implement every instructional strategy under the sun with their staff. The process of determining these practices for each campus is discussed in greater detail in chapter 2.

In implementing an instructional program, it is important to contemplate whom the message should come from. One could argue that it should be led by the principal, the instructional leader of the campus. One of the biggest mistakes made repeatedly on campuses and in districts is relying on outside presenters pushing programs. These presenters spend the day with your staff and are gone the next day. The presentation leaves everyone feeling warm and fuzzy but does not tend to have the staying power one would expect.

Why does that feeling of excitement tend not to last? Much of it has to do with the fact that outside presenters have an incentive to demonstrate their product, whatever form that comes in, as successful. It is how they get paid. These presenters do not know the students at each campus. Students from campus to campus have different instructional needs influenced by economic, cultural, and even geographic factors.

Outside presenters do not know a school's teachers and staff. (Soon to be discussed is how teacher experience affects instruction and shapes a campus.) Frequently, an outside presenter's goal is to make money and peddle a product. It is hard to believe that someone can come in with a fix for whatever problems a campus has without knowing and understanding the specific needs of the students and teachers.

To ensure sustainability, principals should not get caught in the trap of bringing new learning to their campuses prior to being well versed in it themselves. Once the flashy presenter leaves, there are sure to be questions, wrong turns, and wipeouts to navigate throughout the school year. If principals are not well versed in what they bring to a campus, who is going navigate these issues?

To push this situation a little further, take a minute to reflect on teachers' perceptions of the principal in these situations gives teachers. Here they are, with questions and ideas relating to the program the principal brought in, and now that the presenter is gone, the principal does not know what to do. This type of situation hardly inspires teachers to follow the principal's lead.

Let's be clear: Principals should not stop seeking to improve instruction from outside resources. I do not want to discourage the desire to learn with and through others. The message is actually quite the opposite: Principals should be encouraged to seek professional development and be in constant pursuit of better instruction on their campuses. However, the key is that the principals should first gain that knowledge and then bring it back to their staffs. The principal must pursue not only the knowledge but also the plan for sustainability.

No one knows a campus better than the building principal. He should be fully aware of the needs of the students and staff. In addition, as the instructional leader, the principal should know the best way to approach change or improvement to ensure sustainability and success. If in-service activities are designed to improve the needs of the staff, why would we think anyone is better suited for that job than our master teacher, the instructional leader, the principal?

Remember, the principal is held up as a master teacher. When a staff hears the charge from the principal, it carries weight. When teachers see something is important to the principal or when the principal tells them that something is good for kids, it becomes important to teachers, as well. Teachers are not going to give credence to a random presenter who is not going to be there with them when they have questions or when things get tough. When it comes from their leader, someone who knows them and their students, the charge is galvanized.

The other reason outside professional development lacks sustainability, one that is too often forgotten in education, is the importance of follow-through. Our profession is sadly centered on the nonsustaining power of the back-to-school in-service. This is when principals across the country bring out their big guns. Principals give passionate speeches and have flashy activities to rally the troops. Then the school year starts, and teachers go back to their classrooms, administrators return to their offices, and school becomes school again. All of the hoopla and lofty goals give way to the grind.

In the early stages of establishing an instructional program, principals need to focus on one to three manageable, sustainable, and impactful practices that they can emphasize the entire year. A principal should know her staff's weaknesses and attack them. She should be able to explain why she chose a focus and how it is going to help students achieve at greater levels while being ready to defend it when teachers challenge it. Above all, a principal should know her purpose and how it will affect her campus inside and out. Build the hill that you die on if need be. Establish its paramount importance.

I dedicate a significant part of this book to the development and implementation of the instructional program. The one aspect I need to introduce before delving in much further, though, is leadership. If a principal cannot fulfill this requirement, success will be hard to find. If principals are to be successful in their role as instructional leaders, how are they to get people to follow? How do they get teachers to believe in their path for improvement? What makes some principals fail as leaders and others succeed?

All of these are important questions, and there are even more questions that I tackle concerning this idea of leadership. Finding answers to these questions is imperative to campus success and student achievement. The answers are not always as clear as we may like, but in order to have a strong leader as principal, it is necessary to search for them.

The search for those answers begins with the principal interview. People who have participated in a principal interview, either as the interviewer or interviewee, have in some form or fashion come across the leadership question. Everyone aspiring to be in an administrative position has been coached on answering the leadership question, and we all know the buzzwords to use in our answers. The problem is that school districts all over the country choose the wrong people to lead their campuses. Once again, important questions arise:

- Are we asking the right questions?
- Do we have a clear understanding of exactly what we are looking for?

Unfortunately, leadership is a tricky quality to project in interview answers. In order to accomplish all that is covered in this book, a campus must have a true leader at the helm. A true leader is someone who can make a hard decision, someone who has the conviction to ride out an initiative, and someone who can stand up for what is right in the face of adversity. A principal must be able to convey a message and explain it in a way that people can understand while being a visionary who can paint a picture for the future. None of these leadership traits can easily be discerned by yes-or-no questions in an interview.

How can an organization forecast these abilities in an interview lasting sixty minutes? What is the impact on students if the wrong person is hired? The pressure to create a process to ensure success and find the right fit for a campus is immense. Getting this hire wrong can set a campus, and more importantly students, behind significantly, and then the effort required to get things going back in the right direction is also significant.

After all, think about the damage an ineffective principal can inflict on a campus. The obvious major impact is on student learning and achievement. However, what is not as obvious is that low student learning and achievement is often the result of other crucial issues. Ineffective principals lead campuses without direction. Campuses without direction lead to a culture of instructional isolation. Cultures of instructional isolation lead to poor instructional practices.

A principal taking over such a campus is looking at quite an undertaking. All of the above are dire consequences of selecting the wrong person as principal and instructional leader. In chapter 2, I discuss how districts can get more insight into candidates during principal interviews.

But before the interviews start, one must consider what is required of a strong instructional leader as a principal. To gain the trust of a staff, principals must first be master communicators. Gaining trust is sometimes more difficult than expected. We usually think a good communicator is someone who is personable or someone who generally gets along with most people. These traits are good, but the emphasis should be more on the ability to communicate a vision, to easily explain the rationale, and to clearly convey expectations.

When one looks for a quality communicator as principal, one should have some scenarios in mind to guide the search. The instructional leader should be someone who can communicate about change. Change, as already discussed, is a difficult process, but at some point, it will be necessary within any organization. Schools need a principal who can explain a rationale, ease fears, and guide people through a transition.

Another communication facet the instructional leader should have is the ability to communicate a vision. The principal should be able to go beyond the prose of mission and vision statements and break them down to the basics. It is this ability to communicate that can get teachers, parents, and students to jump on the bandwagon. No one is jumping on a road to nowhere. Principals have to show others that they know the way.

During an interview, it is difficult to identify a good communicator. Applicants discuss how great they are as communicators in an interview, but they do so without ever having to listen, which may be the most important part of communication. The people listening in an interview are the people making the decisions. How are our current practices set up to determine a principal applicant's ability to listen and take in information from teachers, staff, and stakeholders? Do our current practices allow us to truly see if principal candidates understand what makes people tick?

Schools need principals who understand that talking *at* people is not always the most effective way of communicating with teachers and staff. Principals who are able to foster more reflective, two-way conversations are usually more successful in reaching desired outcomes. To frame a conversation in this manner is often easier said than done and, as with many topics I discuss, requires a purposeful plan of action.

These kinds of conversations do not just happen off the cuff. The principal's role is much more to facilitate than to dominate the conversation. Principals should go into a conversation with a game plan to help direct the teacher to solutions for an issue. To facilitate a conversation, the principal should form questions that require reflective answers and be ready to react to those answers in a way that encourages teachers to reflect on a solution they can own.

The key to this type of conversation is that, by seemingly stepping back from the situation, the principal gives the ownership of the solution to the teacher. What is perceived as the administrator stepping back from the situation actually may have required more effort on the part of the principal. Many times, it would definitely be easier for principals to just step in and solve the problem, but by adjusting their approach, all involved parties arrive at a thoughtful outcome. In turn, this type of approach by the principal builds trust and ownership with the staff.

Putting the previously mentioned characteristics into practice, especially in the field of education, is about expressing what is important instructionally while hearing input on the many ways instructional strategies can be implemented. Understanding teaching styles is almost as important, if not equally important, as understanding learning styles. Just as in teaching kids and not forcing a square peg into a round hole, principals need to do the same when leading teachers. Principals need to be open to the idea that there may be more than one way to teach students.

Forcing teachers to teach a certain way to ensure principals' comfort levels and their ideas of how the instructional program goals should be met is shortsighted and fails to respect the individual teaching styles of the staff. In doing this, principals are essentially setting teachers up to fail and thereby setting up every student they teach to not meet expectations. Also, by not allowing different teaching styles, principals can shortchange their campus's capacity for instructional growth by limiting the opportunity to learn with and through others new, more efficient ways to achieve instructional goals.

For instance, a principal may have one teacher who works best through controlled chaos. This type of teacher has a classroom where students are everywhere, the atmosphere is messy and rambunctious, and it may possibly drive certain administrators crazy. It may seem on the surface loud and rambunctious, as though there would be zero chance of student learning. However, through formative- and summative-assessment data, a principal could see evidence of a high level of student learning.

On the other hand, a principal may have a teacher who is very organized. This teacher has students sit in rows, and the classroom is a picture of structure on steroids. Some administrators can walk into a classroom like this and find their inner peace. This class may lack student engagement and pizzazz and be orderly, but the students seem about to fall out from boredom. Just as in the other class, though, formative- and summative-assessment data could show that students are learning at high levels.

What can be especially difficult for principals is when a teacher's teaching style is the polar opposite of what their own was like. As a quality instructional leader, principals should not dictate a different mode of instruction simply because a classroom is not what they would consider a model learning environment. At the end of the day, the instructional leader should realize that students are learning at a high level, and that is the ultimate goal.

To further illustrate how principals can handle different teaching styles, I take a look at the practice of "essential questions," which is is a type of formative assessment where the teacher simply asks a question at the end of a lesson cycle to assess the students' knowledge of the day's learning goal. In this illustration, the principal tells teachers on the campus that they are to ask an essential question at the end of the instructional set before moving on to the next subject or class period. With this essential-question directive, the principal is incorporating a new initiative in the instructional program.

Before I explore different approaches to essential questions, keep in mind the following questions:

- Should a principal expect that every teacher execute this practice the same way, avoiding confrontation?
- Is allowing teacher input on the practice inviting a power struggle?
- Is consistency more important than innovation?

As the instructional leader, a principal must ensure that a chosen practice is implemented, but a principal should also reflect on whether the implementation method is always best. Principals need to sometimes accept that there may be a better way.

In the essential-question scenario, a principal has two teachers requesting to move the essential question to different parts of the lesson cycle. The math teacher asks to move it to the end of the guided practice set, before the individual practice set, so that she can do small-group instruction for students who were unsuccessful. The reading teacher wants to move his essential question to the beginning of the class to establish the direction of instruction for the rest of the period based on knowledge retention from the previous day. The principal must determine how to respond to these requests.

There are three common approaches to this scenario. The first has the principal acting as an instructional leader who would ideally take the teacher's input, assess the instructional validity, and allow the teacher to change the process accordingly. This path validates the teacher's role in establishing the practice, builds trust with the teacher, and gives the teacher ownership in the instructional program. All this is accomplished by working jointly, with egos pushed aside, to accomplish what is best for students.

Conversely, a principal making decisions but not as an instructional leader would focus on making sure every teacher is following the rules as instructed, regardless of how the suggestions may improve instruction. This is usually the case when principals are not secure in their role as instructional leaders. The faulty thinking here is that, if the principal allows teachers to change the practice, teachers are essentially going against him, and he is no longer in control. This rationale is more concerned with the principal's perceived power than instructional growth.

The third approach a principal can take, one that is also not a reflection of strong instructional leadership, is to change the practice for every teacher because the change made sense for one teacher. This reaction can at least be considered a good-faith error. In this approach, the principal is acting in a manner that she believes will increase instructional efficacy across the building.

What the instructional leader needs to realize is that no one practice will work the same for everyone. When respecting teaching styles and taking into account variances due to content, one can only expect that teachers may sometimes need the freedom to put their own spin on things. The line of thinking in the third option will keep principals chasing their tails endlessly any time instructional change is implemented.

In the first response to this scenario, the key is for one to be flexible in communicating the expectation while holding fast to one's conviction. When the principal and instructional leader of a campus believes an initiative is good for kids and has background and understanding to communicate the benefit for students, conviction is imperative.

This is because change is hard for everyone, and pushback from the staff is inevitable. Flexibility is also important because, although principals are the instructional leaders of a campus, they are not necessarily always the content experts. Principals must be flexible enough to realize that instructional strategies can be implemented differently to be the most effective between content areas.

In the essential-questions scenario, the first, and most favorable, option results in building trust with the teacher. So, what role does trust play in instructional leadership? Trust may be one of the most, if not the most, important aspects of instructional leadership. As important as it is, the difficulty of achieving it can be extreme. Many leaders make the mistake of trying to force trust and consequently come up short.

How does one go about gaining the trust of a staff of teachers? Gaining the trust of teachers is one of those tasks that many can talk about at length but not as many can truly put into practice. Some principals demand trust, whereas others earn it. It is not hard to imagine which approach works best, as it is highly debatable whether trust can be demanded. However, it has not stopped people from trying.

When a principal implements anything new with teachers, gaining trust is especially important. Teachers will follow someone they believe in, and believing in someone is impossible without trusting that that person has their best interests at heart. There are many missteps administrators make in the pursuit of gaining teachers' trust. Quite often, this is due to the many interpretations of what the teacher-administrator trust relationship looks like and how to build it.

To be clear, when trust is discussed in this book, it refers to a relationship in which honest, two-way conversation transpires between a teacher and an administrator to positively impact classroom instruction. This means that, when a teacher and an administrator have conversations that may be critical in nature, the trust relationship enables the educators to evaluate instruction in a way that allows instruction to be improved without undue friction or hard feelings.

For instance, one principal might be the most beloved person on campus. This kind of principal organizes after-work activities and staff get-togethers at his home and has the reputation of always supporting the teachers. However, student achievement on campus is lower than expected, and instruction is poor in classrooms. When confronted about the situation, this principal states that the staff is working hard and that, with "their group of kids," meeting standards is very difficult.

In this example, the principal has built great relationships with the teachers and staff. The problem is that these types of relationships are not always beneficial for student achievement. This principal built his relationships with a focus on adult friendships instead of on more professional interactions that are student driven. In their professional relationships with their staffs, principals can blend a respect from teachers with the drive for instructional growth, with the key being that the relationship does not get in the way of doing what is best for the students.

Of course, the real challenge is building these types of relationships. In order to foster a relationship where criticism is welcomed, the teacher receiving the criticism needs a great sense of security. How do principals build relationships with teachers that allow them to feel comfortable when being critiqued, which basically means being told you are not doing something well enough?

This is where the principal as an instructional leader earns her keep. It is definitely a difficult task. Throughout this book, I ask more of the principal. Building a level of trust with teachers that allows them to be willing to accept criticism takes nothing more than time and effort. This sounds, at face value, like not that difficult a need to fulfill, but no one understands more than administrators how difficult it is to squeeze blood from a turnip, in terms of making more time.

There are two common ways principals spend time building relationships with teachers. One way fosters a professional type of trust relationship I recommend; the other way focuses on adult friendship, as discussed earlier. Unfortunately, with friendship-focused relationships, it is extremely hard to attain instructional goals. Becoming friends with one's staff makes it incredibly difficult later to provide the staff honest, constructive criticism.

As I advocate avoiding friendship relationships to gain favor and personal gratification, what is sometimes overlooked is that principals can still spend time knowing their staffs on a personal level while maintaining work-focused relationships driven by student achievement. These relationships are built with the expectation of constructive conversation surrounding instruction and student achievement. The question principals need to ask themselves is whether their current relationships with their staffs encourage or deter the crucial conversations required of an instructional leader.

At the end of the day, teachers need to feel their principal is in it with them. They want to see that their instructional leader's abilities allow her to be capable of providing quality feedback on the instructional practices she is asking them to implement when she is in their classrooms. The key is to understand the difference between *criticizing* and *evaluating* instructional practices.

When a principal is critically reviewing a teacher's instructional practice, it almost seems as though the principal's goal is to find something the teacher is doing wrong. This creates negative feelings in the teacher-administrator relationship. Evaluating instructional practices means being an advocate for teachers during the process. In this advocate role, the principal is supporting and coaching the teacher by providing pointers and advice along the way.

A supportive instructional leader fosters an environment that allows the teachers to feel free to make mistakes or take risks. This is because they understand that the principal is anticipating a learning curve. They will have learned through the principal's leadership that stepping outside of their comfort zones may lead to a more effective practice than could be found otherwise.

This environment enables teachers to push themselves without fear of adverse consequences. This is essential to the process because, in order get familiar with a new practice, teachers need to know that failures will be accepted and that those failures will not reflect poorly on them when administrators come in for coaching visits. In the end, how can teachers expect to improve without trying something new, and how can principals expect them to try something new if they foster a culture in which teachers fear doing so?

Up to this point, the principal's roles and how they work to support teachers to facilitate high-quality instruction in every classroom have been discussed at length. If we were to meld all the instructional roles and responsibilities of the principal into one quintessential task, it would be to ensure that the campus is staffed with highly effective teachers. As stated earlier, the teacher has the most direct impact on student achievement. If we believe this to be so, it is the ultimate responsibility of the principal as the instructional leader to hire, train, and maintain the best staff possible.

If we can accept that building a staff of highly effective teachers is the most important responsibility of principals, what are the implications of not being successful in this endeavor? The reality is that the responsibility for poor instruction lays at the feet of the campus principal. So how do principals handle this immense responsibility? To hire highly effective teachers, an administrator must be familiar with certain aspects of hiring.

Before I go into these aspects, I should establish that a principal must be able to evaluate hiring practices and to understand that there are different tiers of teacher experience. Among those tiers, there should be different sets of expectations and different levels of support to adequately help teachers and ensure their success. Understanding this premise will be the baseline of evaluating hiring practices, as it will help in identifying the support each teacher requires to be successful.

Going into the interview process, principals must have a clear understanding of what exactly they view the job of teachers to be. What is in the job description we should require of teachers? In the hiring process, all of the buzzwords are discussed: formative assessment, summative assessment, scaffolding, spiraling, engagement, higher-level learning, rigor. The list goes on and on. We talk about these things until we are blue in the face, but do we discuss what they look, taste, smell, feel, and sound like?

We have all heard the stories of colleagues taking on campuses who are shocked by the skills the staffs do not have or the essential understandings that are not present. Picture a principal leading an in-service and asking teachers to compare formative and summative assessments; all the principal sees are blank stares. Another dismaying example is in interviews when teachers are asked how they check for understanding, and they respond with "homework."

One element of bringing in quality teachers that must be discussed is how we evaluate teachers during the interview process. In many occupations, interviews require applicants to demonstrate the job-embedded skills that will be required of them in the positions they are applying for. As educators, we ask a lot of questions to help us evaluate how applicants would perform the skills required to be effective teachers.

The problem with the traditional question-and-answer interview model is that this process goes nowhere near allowing us to project the kind of teacher the applicants truly are. Anyone who has been part of the hiring process from the other side of the desk knows that both strong and weak teachers can answer the questions traditionally asked, thereby relegating the process to a fifty-fifty proposition at best.

Those doing the hiring have all kinds of methods to their madness. Many times, people hire based on the personality of the applicant or on the interviewer's gut feeling. Teachers know what is supposed to happen in the classroom, but executing it in a way that generates enough enthusiasm in students is a special trait that cannot be addressed through a question-and-answer session.

So, if administrators are going about it all wrong, what is the solution? The answer may very well be that there is no end-all-be-all solution. However, getting close to the answer entails finding ways each campus or district can get more tangible evidence from principal-teacher interviews. Indeed, getting closer to the answer might be in finding more ways that allow principals to quit relying on their guts or on anecdotal evidence conjured by feelings they get about an applicant from antiquated questions.

Rather than throw this out there and leave everyone to their own devices, there is, of course, one interesting approach to drive a more job-skill-embedded interview process for teachers. Why could we not put a teacher in a classroom full of kids as part of the interview? A principal could schedule the interview three days in advance and let the applicant know what learning standard he would be teaching and the resources available in the classroom and wish him luck.

Take a step back and think about this for a minute. Instead of asking applicants how they keep students engaged and getting some pat answer in return, principals could see if they can actually keep a class full of students engaged. The same can be said for any range of instructional skills principals traditionally ask candidates about in the interview process. This outside-the-box interview style allows the interviewer to truly evaluate a candidate's instructional practices, as opposed to just hearing what she can tell principals about them.

For an example, the instructional leader has identified a specific campus weakness and has begun interviewing teacher applicants. Through the skill-embedded interview, teachers can demonstrate in a real-life classroom whether they would be an asset to the school. In addition, the principal could see which teachers had strengths in the needed area in a way that could not be identified through interview questions. Interviews of this style eliminate the missing factor of hiring someone really good at talking the talk but incapable of walking the walk.

Another aspect principals must understand during the interview process is that not all teachers are created equal. Principals should carefully consider the type of teacher they are looking for to fill campus needs. For example, at one point, a principal may be in need of a teacher with experience, one who has been battle tested and can offer a mentoring role for the staff. At another time, the principal may be at a school that has a solid core of teachers and feels comfortable supporting the needs of a teacher fresh out of college. Yet there are other situations where the principal may just need fresh ideas and may be looking for a teacher with three to five years of experience. There may be times when the principal is looking for certain combinations to fit the needs of the campus. The key is to have a plan.

For the purpose of this discussion, note that schools have three groups of teachers: novice, experienced, and veteran. A novice teacher is obviously brand new to the education profession, either straight from college or as a second-career teacher from an alternative certification program. Generally, an experienced teacher has three to five years of experience. This group of teachers is beginning to feel confident that they are figuring things out. The veteran teacher has six-plus years of experience. This group of teachers brings the skins on the wall.

Principals must understand that growing teachers without knowing the different needs of teachers within these groups is poor practice, as teachers within these groups require different growth plans. In other words, growing a teacher does not work using a one-size-fits-all model because teachers within these groups should be handled differently throughout the growth and evaluation process. The criteria that principals use to do the unenviable job on deciding to move forward with or move on from a teacher also vary within the experience groups.

The following account illustrates how the teachers in these different experience groups would be viewed. How often have administrators heard teachers say, "I taught it; I don't know why they don't get it"? It's the old "You can lead a horse to water, but you can't make it drink" adage. Unfortunately, it is not uncommon to hear this statement in schools. But what is interesting is what this statement tells us about teachers. This is a loaded statement, and it tells administrators more than one may think. It should be heard and interpreted differently among the teachers in the different experience groups.

The first thing it does for principals is gives them an idea of what some educators perceive their job to be. I discussed earlier what principals should view a teacher's job to be, but by making this statement, the teacher is telling the principal how the teacher views the job. The teacher who makes this statement believes that a teacher's job is to simply present material. That is, if the teacher presents the material in a way he believes to be high quality, students should learn. This misperception of what a teacher's job is leads to a deeply flawed instructional plan that drastically inhibits student achievement.

This rationale would not be very surprising from a novice teacher. This type of instructional plan of simply presenting material is by far the easiest to execute: the teacher teaches; the student learns. By most accounts, this is the type of setting most novice teachers straight from college have been in for the better part of four years. As the instructional leader, a principal should not view this response the same way as one from a teacher in one of the other experience groups. It is important to intervene swiftly, though. The principal should view it as a coaching opportunity.

The great thing about novice teachers is that they do not have bad habits the principal has to retrain at this point. However, by not intervening appropriately in a timely manner, the principal encourages bad practices to become habits that will be exponentially harder to deal with later. Novice teachers simply need coaching, guidance, and quality feedback with the expectations of quality instruction. Novice teachers, like everyone else, are going to fall back on what they know. The problem is that they do not have any experience on which to fall back. Simply put, they need the principal to give them some tricks for their bag.

When considering this response from an experienced teacher, we must remember we are speaking of that teacher who is in the three to five years of experience range. Therefore, what is needed to grow the experienced teacher is different from that of a novice teacher. A response of this nature from an experienced teacher should make the principal a little edgy. At that point, the principal should explain that this thought process is unacceptable. An instructional leader in this situation then begins the process of analyzing the teacher's instructional plan and facilitating conversations to get the instruction back on a suitable path.

The growth piece at this level is one where the principal must begin the process of helping the teacher "unlearn" bad instructional habits. To start, the principal should assess the teacher's understanding of formative-assessment practices. The real issue here is determining whether the teacher is capable of changing her stripes in terms of bad habits. Old habits are hard to break, and the teacher has to be willing to change. Part of understanding change is accepting that change is needed. This is another example of a heavy-lifting task for the instructional leader.

A veteran teacher using this rationale should bring real fear to the principal. First, veteran teachers, whether the principal wants them to be or not, are frequently the statesmen of the campus. These teachers are often the ones many other teachers go to for advice and help. In fact, until the principal has developed a culture where teachers truly trust her, the veteran teacher is always going to be a less intimidating source of help. The problem arises when the statesman's instruction is poor and he is who everyone turns to for advice. Inevitably, the instruction in the building will be poor.

Another reason a principal should be concerned by a veteran teacher's poor advice is that often these are the teachers who are most set in their ways. During meetings that include veteran teachers, the principal had better come prepared because they will be the ones to challenge new lines of thinking on instruction. This situation can go one of two ways. If the principal is not comfortable instructionally, the skeptical veteran teacher will eat the principal alive. In turn, this will likely cause the principal to lose credibility with the teacher and others on the staff. On top of that, the principal risks entering into a very open power struggle with a subordinate.

On the other hand, if a principal can convert veteran teachers, they can potentially be his most trusted instructional allies. Veteran teachers are not in the profession for the riches and fame. Veteran teachers are almost always in the business for the kids they work with. If a principal can show them how and why an instructional practice is better for kids and that it increases student achievement, he will get the veteran teachers onboard, with everyone who comes to them jumping on the bandwagon, as well.

Just as a quality teacher in a classroom is essential to student achievement, an instructional leader as the principal is essential to the overall success of the school. Principals are responsible for all aspects of the instructional program for a campus, from setting expectations to maintaining staff. Maintaining staff includes hiring, dismissing, and training. So once again, if we are to accept all the data on the importance of the teacher in the classroom, we must recognize the importance of the principal as instructional leader in being responsible for those teachers.

The benefit of having the right teacher in the classroom is undeniable. Of equal, or arguably more, importance is having the right principal in the building. As important as the teacher is, the principal as the instructional leader drives the quality of the teachers in the building. This responsibility reaches across hiring, retaining, and training. Principals are also responsible for the instructional program the teachers implement in every classroom. Every organization needs a strong leader, and schools are no different.

SUMMARY

The importance of the teacher in the classroom is well documented, and data to that fact does not lie. What we also need to realize, though, is the importance of the principal to the teacher in the classroom. Educators need to quickly realize that times are changing, and quality principals as instructional leaders are as essential to schools as water is to the human body. The days of the principal as the manager of the school are long behind us. Principals today need be the master teacher while wearing all the traditional hats that keep the job interesting. The principalship is much more than it has ever been, and those looking to pursue the big chair need to be ready, eyes wide open, because this is not the job it used to be; it is much, much more!

THREE POINTS TO REMEMBER

1. The teacher has the highest impact on student achievement in the classroom, but the principal is responsible for hiring quality teachers.
2. The principal is also responsible for training quality teachers.
3. The principal is also responsible for retaining quality teachers.

Chapter Two

Instruction—What's the Difference between Talking the Talk and Walking the Walk?

Many of us remember school as when the teacher's job was to teach, and the student's job was to listen and learn. There was generally some homework, and then it was time to rinse and repeat the next day. School is not the same as it used to be. Students are not the same as they used to be. Today's students have more going on in their lives outside of school than today's adults ever did. The average American family does not come together every evening and sit down for dinner at 5:00 p.m. anymore, followed by homework time and an 8:00 p.m. bedtime.

This realization presents instructional leaders with many things to think about and address. First, they must realize that they are in direct competition for students' time. They are competing with sports, cell phones, and reality TV in addition to all the other time-honored pastimes they have always competed with. This is a real issue because relying on students to focus on academics outside of the school day, as in the past, is no longer an option due to the increasing amount of tasks taking up their time once the last bell rings at school.

Second, due to various factors, such as dual-income families or even a devalued appreciation of education, we do not have the parental support we were accustomed to in generations past. Regardless of the reason, parents are not as available to students as they used to be. Even when parents are available to help their children with academics, many do not feel competent in some of the content of our higher-level courses.

Finally, as already discussed, kids change. Schools are welcoming new kids every year who are increasingly different from the kids we were in school. This concept may be the most difficult for educators to take on. This requires us to adapt to our students rather than the students adapting to us. It is our job as instructional leaders to recognize that times are changing and we must adapt.

This realization magnifies the importance of the time we actually have with the kids. The time we get has become a treasured commodity, and it should be treated as such. Instructional leaders must ensure that instructional time is efficient and productive and that its success is measured every day. Principals must create instructional programs that focus on three things:

- teachers knowing what they are doing
- teacher knowing how to measure success
- teachers knowing how to interpret data

In the first chapter, I establish that the teacher has the greatest effect on student achievement in the classroom, but the principal is responsible for hiring and developing good teachers. This line of thinking establishes the principal as having the greatest impact on student achievement at the campus level and essentially places the quality of instruction, good or bad, at the feet of the principal.

This responsibility clearly places the principal as the instructional alpha leader, in a matter of speaking. We need to flesh out what it means to be an instructional leader and how to find one. It seems as though anyone can throw around any of the infinite buzzwords that are associated with instructional leadership, but do all of these people understand how to incorporate these buzzwords into actual instructional leadership?

Imagine you are the principal and are walking into the building for the first day of the back-to-school in-service. You have the most brilliant, well-conceived plan to review the use of formative and summative assessment on your campus. Twenty minutes into your presentation, the questions start flying. Teachers are asking if what they are currently doing fits into what you are asking for and if what they are doing is right or wrong, and it hits you: you do not have the answers.

What impression are you sending to your staff as the instructional leader, the person they are supposed to look up to? You have just presented yourself as the instructional leader, the master teacher, and here you are, unable to answer their questions concerning the instructional plan you are bringing to the campus. Make no mistake about it: the message you have sent is definitely that you are severely lacking.

Just like the saying about kids being able to smell a fake, the same is true of teachers during an in-service. If principals are going to be successful as instructional leaders, they must be able to demonstrate their mastery of instruction. Principals must have the answers in defense of their instructional programs against any argument. Also, they must be able to communicate the validity of their programs in the face of all data sets. Of all people, principals need to be able to walk the walk instructionally.

One of the primary responsibilities of the principal as the instructional leader is establishing the instructional program for the campus. As I have discussed, this is by no means a small task. To be successful in such a huge undertaking, there is a great deal of work required. Identifying the wrong person for this position will lead to student achievement levels below expectations. Therefore, principals carry a heavy burden as decision makers.

An essential trait in being able to create and implement a quality instructional program is knowing and understanding what quality instruction looks like in a classroom. Principals should be able to both discuss and apply instruction, thereby talking the talk and walking the walk. When choosing principals to lead a campus as the instructional leader, their instructional ability should be unquestioned.

This description does not seem like a lot to ask, but when searching for quality principals, we stack the deck against ourselves sometimes by making a series of assumptions about candidates based on their backgrounds and the jargon they use. In turn, this makes the process of finding a great principal incredibly difficult. Everyone knows the old saying about assumptions, and its punch line could not be any truer in this case.

Instructional program refers to the principal's plan for everything involving instruction on the campus. This includes but is not limited to how the principal wants teachers to conduct assessments, both formative and summative. Also, the principal should establish how often those assessments are to be given. In fact, the principal's instructional plan should detail things as minor as how questioning should be practiced in classrooms. Essentially, the principal should identify the core instructional practices to maximize student achievement in the building.

To be successful in this task, principals must choose what they deem to be the fundamental instructional practices for which they are willing to die on the hill. These are the core practices that will be drilled, discussed, and then drilled again. These practices are not necessarily trendy or the kind that explode on the scene in the education world. Instructional leaders are looking for practices that are rooted in data and proven to increase student achievement and learning. As programs and technologies come and go, these fundamental practices will stand the test of time.

The whole point in implementing fundamental instructional practices is that they are applicable to any content area in the building. In other words, a principal's fundamental practices should be just as effective in a band class as in a math class. This concept should not be difficult for instructional leaders to wrap their minds around, as quality instructional practices should be universal, regardless of content.

These practices require buy-in from everyone in the building. All the teachers at the campus should know that these established practices are to be observed in every classroom and why they are important. Indeed, teachers should understand how implementing these fundamental practices helps make them better teachers, thereby making their students more successful learners.

When creating an instructional program, there are many steps that must be taken to determine the direction it should take. An instructional leader must inventory a staff's knowledge of such things as assessment practices, both formative and summative; the teachers' instructional abilities; and any curricular needs, such as the quality of scope and sequences. Some of the worst mistakes principals make, especially new principals, are creating instructional plans without assessing the lay of the land and implementing change simply for the sake of change.

For example, when you visit the doctor, before she hands you a diagnosis and prescription, she checks your vitals, looks for telling symptoms, and does a general screening of your overall health. Principals must do the same by thoroughly examining their campuses before they are able to establish an instructional program. It would be a foolhardy endeavor to walk onto a campus and begin putting practices in place prior to assessing the staff's abilities, taking an inventory of what is currently in place, and identifying problems.

Practically speaking, examining a campus is going to require time. It starts with the principal being in classrooms and having instructional conversations with teachers. When principals are in classrooms, they should note how their concept of fundamental instructional practices are being implemented. Principals may notice that some of those practices are not being implemented at all. Principals should observe the strengths and weaknesses of the instruction in order to determine the growth areas that should be given the highest priority.

During discussions with teachers, the principal should find out where they are coming from instructionally. That is, are they willing and able, shell-shocked, or set in bad habits? The principal should determine if there are unwritten rules or a climate impeding quality instructional practices that may need to be considered. The principal's conversations with teachers may uncover the "why" for much of what is observed, allowing for a better understanding of how to proceed.

The staff inventory is essential to the success of any instructional plan's implementation. In order to identify the jumping-off point, a principal must know where to begin. For instance, it would be important to know the staff's understanding of general practices, like formative and summative assessment. Knowing if the staff is able to differentiate between formative and summative assessment, if they have a good understanding of each, will be critical to the principal's next steps.

It would also be good to know where the teachers are in terms of understanding data. Teachers able to disaggregate their formative- and summative-assessment data will be more effective in adjusting instruction to meet the needs of their students. With data analysis, trying to implement too much too fast may lead to false information driving instructional decisions. Attempting to push the staff too far without their having the prerequisite skills will result in the failure of a principal's instructional program and quite possibly a significant drop in morale, leading to a drop in trust.

As part of the initial inventory, the principal should also be looking for things that are working well toward an instructional plan. If the campus is strong in formative and summative practices, there is no need to work at a novice level. Indeed, the principal may be pleased to find that the teachers are implementing quality instructional practices in ways heretofore not done by the principal. After all, there is always someone out there doing it better; we cannot limit ourselves, blinders on, only seeing things our way because doing something different may take us out of our comfort zones.

Once a principal has created the instructional plan and galvanized fundamental practices on a campus, implementation is the next focus. The key to this phase is communication of the instructional program. The principal as an instructional leader needs to know how to make instruction a priority on the campus. Principals should realize that, for instruction to be seen as important, the staff needs to see its importance from the top. A good principal knows this is not accomplished through edicts and demands but through collaborative efforts that foster a feeling of shared duty.

To show a staff how important instruction is, a principal must live, eat, and breathe instruction. When this is happening, the staff is almost surprised if they do not have some sort of instructional conversation when they see the principal in the hallways. The staff understands that the principal celebrates instruction and that instruction drives the principal's campus goals and expectations.

Instruction is definitely not something the principal talks about once at the beginning of the year or at a couple faculty meetings. Instead, the principal discusses instruction repeatedly throughout the school year. People know what is important to principals by what they spend their time doing. The same can be said about what they spend their time talking about.

In order to foster this culture of instruction, the instructional leader must be the campus expert when it comes to all things instruction. Just as people jump on a plane with the utmost confidence in the pilot to fly the plane, the staff wants to have the same confidence in the principal to run the instructional program for the school. There cannot be a belief among the staff the principal cannot fly the plane.

In addition, an instructional leader should be confident in instructional practices across content areas. This is important because strong instructional leaders have the responsibility to address instructional deficiencies regardless of the classroom they are observing. Teacher observations may require most of a principal's time and effort; indeed, there is more to this task than most people understand. Success or failure in addressing instructional deficiencies oftentimes determines the fate of instructional leaders and their campuses.

So how are instructional leaders expected to handle a poor lesson given by a teacher? There really is not a clear answer for all situations. The first step, and maybe the most important one, is for the principal to simply discuss any concerns about the lesson with the teacher. A principal cannot ignore or, worse, make excuses for the poor lesson. The hard part in addressing the elephant in the room is deciding how to move forward. As the instructional leader, the principal has to decide what the conversation looks like. The biggest mistake an instructional leader can make is to address the situation without a plan.

In planning for these types of discussions, it is important to go back to the experience groups examined in chapter 1 and determine which one the teacher is in. Quite likely, principals are not going to address the novice teacher the same way they would a veteran teacher. It may not always seem fair, but principals should have higher expectations for teachers who have more experience. Remember, novice teachers do not have nearly as many tricks in their bags as more experienced teachers. For this reason, principals expect more from the more experienced teachers.

The next step in preparing for teacher feedback is to identify what went wrong. Going into the meeting and telling the teacher that the lesson was poor and stating a directive that it needs to get better will not benefit anyone. As the instructional leader and master teacher, it is the principal's responsibility to indicate what needs to be improved to create a more successful lesson. A principal must not only be able to diagnose the issues but also be ready to provide guidance to address those issues.

As discussed earlier, how teachers perceive the feedback depends a great deal on how it is delivered by the principal. Look at the differences between these principal dialogues:

> Principal A: Hello, Mrs. Smith. When I walked through your class today, I was not real impressed with your lesson. The students were not engaged, and you seemed to be up there lecturing the entire time. Next time I come by, I would like to see you asking more questions and doing a better job of formative assessment. That is, I want you to check for student understanding of what you are lecturing about. Do you understand what I am talking about?

Now let us look at a far different approach:

> Principal B: Hello, Mrs. Smith. How do you think the lesson that I observed today went? *(Allow for teacher response.)*

> Principal B: I know we have spent a lot of time this year discussing formative-assessment strategies; how do you think your formatives went during this lesson? *(Allow for teacher response.)*

Principal B: I understand that getting to the formative-assessment piece can be difficult while trying to ensure everything gets covered, but remember, if we teach it and they do not learn it, we are not doing our job. Would it be helpful for me to run through some of your lessons with you before you teach them to find ways to fit the formatives into your lesson cycle? *(Allow for teacher response.)*

Principal B: Great! We can meet during your conference tomorrow and get to work. Also, if there is another teacher you would like to observe to see how they work formatives into their lesson cycle, let me know, and I will get that arranged.

There are several points to consider in comparing the two dialogues. One of the most important is that the second approach is actually a dialogue. In the first dialogue, Principal A is talking *at* the teacher, not *with* the teacher. This is an important distinction because this approach lacks any opportunity for ownership in the discussion by the teacher. Principal A is simply telling the teacher what the perceived issue was and how to go about fixing it. Unfortunately, this opinion is strictly from the principal's point of view and does not allow the teacher any input.

On the other hand, Principal B poses questions that encourage dialogue, or a two-way conversation. The teacher is forced to recognize the issue but also to be a part of the solution. Through this mode of communication, the teacher can explain the rationale behind the lesson and be an active participant in remedying the situation by seeking guidance and clarity. This approach also fosters a culture where both parties work together to find solutions to the issues rather than the principal advocating a top-down approach to instructional growth.

Principal B is able to confront the issue at hand in the classroom without having to establish himself as right and the teacher as wrong. In not engaging in this struggle, the principal demonstrates that it is a collaborative effort. By asking teachers to evaluate the lesson themselves during feedback sessions, the principal is providing the opportunity for teachers to own the situation and evaluate their lessons themselves before the principal has to say anything.

More times than not, the teachers are perfectly aware of whether a lesson was good or bad. Allowing them the opportunity to explain why they think things went awry is powerful for both the teacher and instructional leader. It spurs teachers to consider how to improve future lessons and lets the principal know they are truly going to work through the issue. In this way, the teachers are able to demonstrate that they are aware it is a collaborative effort.

Another way to accomplish this is by asking questions that imply positive intent. When Principal B asks, "How do you think your formatives went during this lesson?" she is not reprimanding the teacher for not seeing something, but once again, through implying positive intent, she allows the teacher to own the situation. The teacher is forced to review his practices and reflect on the implementation or lack thereof.

Toward the end of the teacher feedback, the instructional leader offers assistance. In our examples, Principal A takes the easy road, which is to state the issue and expect the teacher to fix the problem. In contrast, Principal B not only offers assistance but also provides more than one option for the teacher to seek improvement. Notice that both options for help in the second example will require additional time from Principal B, but feedback without support will likely result in failure to see change.

One last aspect to point out is that conversations with teacher feedback should be a process. They should not be done in passing or done quickly between class periods. Conversations of this nature take focused planning, knowledge of instructional practices, and familiarity with the staff. Take a moment to reflect on how a teacher would internalize the conversations from the examples with Principals A and B. What perceptions of the principal and the instructional culture on a campus come out of each of these conversations, and what are the ramifications of those perceptions?

Having discussed how to frame instructional conversations, let us explore some common practical scenarios of teachers in need. In the first scenario, a principal is conducting a walk-through evaluation on a quality veteran teacher and observes the teacher asking amazing questions of the students. The questions are at a rigorous level, there are great follow-up questions, and the responses are student driven. On the surface, everything seems to be going well. However, there is still more information the principal needs for his evaluation.

In breaking down the teacher's questioning practices, the principal notices that the teacher was only calling on the students who were raising their hands. It is a common practice for teachers to assess achievement of a learning goal by the number of hands raised. It would be easy for the principal to praise the teacher for the expert-level questioning and move on to the next task. However, taking the easy road in this case misses out on an amazing coaching opportunity that the principal as an instructional leader should never pass on, one where the instruction in this teacher's classroom could significantly improve.

In this scenario, the principal should celebrate the questioning practices of the teacher, thus reaffirming that quality questioning is an excellent form of formative assessment. Following the praise, the principal should explain how only calling on students who raise their hands eliminates the formative-assessment opportunity from students who are not raising their hands.

As an instructional leader, the principal should be able to communicate that it is specifically the students not raising their hands whom educators need to hear from the most. Unfortunately, these are the types of students educators typically allow to opt out of instruction. Teachers have to be made aware of this reality so that the process of change can begin in the classrooms.

Opting out of instruction is the unintentional by-product of poor instructional practices that allows students to choose not to participate in classroom instruction. Teachers perpetuate opting out of instruction when they only call on students who have their hands raised. When this happens, reluctant learners quickly realize that, if they keep their hands down, then they will not have to participate. In turn, lack of participation often leads to limited student growth. This by-product of poor instructional practice may be one of the more detrimental issues affecting students in our classrooms.

Besides discussing options on how the instructional leader can handle certain scenarios, I also discuss the negative culture potentially resulting from each scenario. The goal is obviously not only to show the decision process but also to illustrate what may happen if the poor instructional practice is left unchecked. In this instance, I discuss the culture we create by enabling students to opt out of instruction through poor questioning practices.

Again, the students we allow to opt out of instruction are typically our reluctant learners. Reluctant learners opt out because they are not confident in their abilities, the content, or both. These students are not willingly going to reach out for help during the learning process. Thus, we cannot afford to allow our instructional practices to provide these opt-out opportunities.

We cannot let our poor, possibly lazy questioning practices continue to foster this opt-out culture. To change this culture, instructional leaders must undo ages of bad practice, as our questioning practices have become institutionalized. The next chapter describes at length how, through a minor shift in strategy, we can radically work toward undoing poor questioning techniques.

This leads us to our next scenario, which concerns the increasingly popular practice of group work. Group work is popular because, if implemented correctly, it can be a very positive instructional practice. The skill of working with others in a group setting has been identified by many as one our students will need to be successful in the twenty-first-century workforce. It is also an instructional setting that can be a booby trap for unsuspecting teachers.

Teachers can take advantage of this increasingly popular practice and thereby sabotage instructional efforts if the principal does not ensure that the practice is implemented soundly. When done correctly, group work requires a great deal of planning and diligent, active monitoring by the teacher. On the negative side is the tendency of teachers to throw students into a group, give them an assignment, and then leave the learning up to chance, all in the guise of cooperative learning.

In our scenario, during walk-through visits, as the principal, you observe students in one classroom working in groups of three to four on an assignment. As you monitor the room, two groups in particular catch your attention. While checking whether every student is actively participating equally, you immediately see that one group has major problems.

In this group, you note one student doing all the work while the other students are talking about something off topic. In thinking back on their school days, everyone can relate to this situation. Indeed, everyone brings up this situation as the major concern with group work. It is this dynamic that drastically devalues the practice's overall effectiveness.

In contrast, the second group that draws your attention is doing everything asked of them. Each student has a specific job and section of the content they are responsible for, and they will each present their assigned sections to the class. As you wrap up your walk-through, you ask the teacher how he is going to assess the students' understanding of the material. The response you get is that he will be assessing their presentations. Everything seems to be in order with this second group, but there is a subtle yet critical coaching issue to discuss with the teacher.

To address this scenario, the first coachable moment for the principal as the instructional leader is discussing how to establish group-work guidelines that reflect sound instructional practice. The goal is to do so without becoming so restrictive that there is not enough variance between content areas and teaching style, where the unintended effect of our feedback is the limited effectiveness of the practice as a whole. Creating a situation of this restrictive nature essentially discourages the use of the practice campus-wide. This is obviously not desirable because group work, when used properly, can be a powerful instructional practice.

Therefore, setting guidelines and expectations for what we do not want group work to be is more beneficial. For teachers, this route allows everyone to work within the framework of both their content areas and teaching styles to maximize the effectiveness of group work in their classroom. For the principal, it establishes parameters that include formative assessment and student accountability.

This group-work scenario also provides opportunities for the principal to discuss the differences between directly and indirectly opting out of instruction. Of course, the students who are off task, causing one student to do all the work, are *directly opting out of instruction*. The obvious goal is that all students be actively participating in group work. To accomplish this, teachers must plan for it.

The number of student-learning tasks must be adequate so that each student has enough to do in the time allotted for the activity. Active monitoring by the teacher is essential, but honestly, this should not have to be spelled out to the teacher. If it has to be, the teacher might have even larger issues than bad instructional practices with group work. Teachers cannot use group work as an opportunity to get work done at their desks.

The more critical issue of the two, but the one we do not always pick up on, was actually happening in the second group, where everyone was working. The students in the second group are *indirectly* opting out of instruction. This is because the group dynamic established by the teacher encourages, or even forces, students to opt out. The teacher has inadvertently made parts of the content only available to certain students, making the often erroneous assumption that the students will just learn from the presentations of other students.

When allowing students to be autonomous in their learning in group-work settings, it is still the responsibility of the teacher to assess whether students are learning the material. Making the assumption that students are actually listening to all the other student presentations, with the added assumption that they learned the learning objective for the activity, may be a bit of a stretch, which most teachers would not be willing to bet their paychecks on. Adding a formative-assessment piece to this group-work activity essentially holds all students accountable for all parts of the content.

Another frequently made mistake is that educators often get too cute with group work. That is, they allow students' talking together and "enjoying" the learning process to pull the wool over their eyes, leading them to falsely believe they are implementing high-level cooperative learning environments. This could not be further from the truth in the scenario just laid out. Sadly, this is what group work looks like on many campuses, and it is not the exception to the rule.

In this kind of group work, the crippling culture we promote is *flash* over *substance*. Through poor walk-though practices, and sometimes praising the product over the level of instruction, principals have been communicating the wrong message to teachers for many years. Flash is nice and can often get students excited about their work. This can definitely be a good thing, especially with the students today. But ultimately, as principals, we need to make sure we praise student learning and achievement first and not lesson products.

In another scenario, in a similar walk-through setting, the principal observes a teacher with very strong content knowledge. This teacher discusses the subject matter at a very deep level that would challenge anyone in her field. In fact, she talks during the entire period and does not hear from one student. Sometimes, the students even seem to be engaged and interested in the lecture.

However, on other days, all the content knowledge in the world is not going to keep the attention of students. These are the days when educators are throwing away instructional time, the time for which we are fighting tooth and nail. On these days, the instructional leader must step in and coach teachers with all the great content knowledge to use other instructional skills to make sure they reach their kids every day.

After all, consider that, when doing a presentation, one usually presumes that the participants have chosen to attend. As administrators, we often pay a lot for registration fees at conferences across the nation. However, the difference with students in schools is that most of the participants would rather be doing something else if given the choice. How, then, does the instructional leader deal with the issue of the presenter versus the teacher?

To answer that question, instructional leaders must be aware of two variables. The first variable is understanding their teachers' backgrounds. As classroom participants when they were in school, many teachers were compliant, goal oriented, and motivated toward success. For many educators, when they were students, things came easily, and they may have even enjoyed the rigors of school. They likely enjoyed reading and buying school supplies and lost sleep in anticipation of the first day of school. Thus, educators' experiences and predispositions often cloud their perceptions of what their students are bringing with them to the classroom.

So how does this disconnect impact the classroom? First, it works to mislead teachers when they are planning instruction. People often teach the way they learn; many teachers assume every student is a sponge, willing and ready to learn each and every day, as they were. This misperception perpetuates the "presenting" model, whereby teachers make the assumption that, as long as they teach it, the students will learn it. Unfortunately, as the adage goes, you can drag a horse to water, but you cannot make it drink.

The second variable is that the instructional leader must realize that teachers are in a battle for students' time. Outside of the school day, students are busier than they ever have been. This is an issue because educators now have to make the forty-five minutes in each class period the most efficient ever just to keep up. If we are to be successful in educating today's student, the days of teachers being the sage on the stage, enjoying the sounds of their own voices, must be over.

So, going back to the scenario where the teacher with great knowledge solely lectures, there are essentially two coaching points for the principal as the instructional leader. First, she needs to have a coaching conversation with the teacher to discuss how he is checking for understanding. That is, what formative assessments is the teacher using to determine the effectiveness of the lecture?

It is not that lecturing is a bad practice, but there still has to be multiple checks for understanding throughout the lecture. The formative assessments I refer to do not require formal activities, and the suggestion is that they stay simple. Teachers need to ask themselves if the students are able to take the knowledge teachers are imparting and apply it in various settings.

The second coaching point is that principals should communicate to the teachers the increasing importance of the forty-five minutes they get each class period and the necessity to make that precious time count. It bears repeating: in this fight for students' time, the forty-five-minute class period is the only time teachers are guaranteed to have. This means the days of the teacher as presenter are over. If the principal walks into a classroom and the teacher is doing all the talking, we have a big problem.

If a principal hires a teacher, it means that he is comfortable with the teacher's content knowledge and does not need to hear how much the teacher knows throughout a forty-five-minute class period. We need to hear from the kids in the classroom. The only way to know if the students are learning is to hear what that they have to say. Indeed, we need to be working on increasing student talk, a topic that is illustrated in detail in the next chapter.

Giving the floor to students is often very difficult for teachers because they are control freaks by nature. When teachers are doing all the talking, they are in control. They control the pace, the amount of content being covered, and the activities. In many of their minds, releasing control of the classroom could result in any number of cataclysms. However, it is paramount that principals coach teachers through this process and communicate the benefits it will provide to their instruction and assessment of student learning.

Knowing which experience group teachers fall into will help principals confront each teacher with the goal of increasing student talk. With a novice teacher, principals are back to programming. Novice teachers want the principal to show them how it is done. This is the opportunity for the principal to train, providing the teacher with the how and the why. Principals should let novice teachers know that having a classroom centered on student talk lends itself naturally to formative assessment, thereby allowing the teachers the opportunity to see if they are truly being effective.

When a principal pushes increased student talk with the experienced teachers, there may be some need to break bad habits. On the plus side, the teachers in this group can reflect on past experiences. They still remember what it was like to be a new teacher and have had their share of victories and failures. As the principal, you can use those to your benefit. Your experienced teachers are more likely to try new strategies because they have built some confidence in their abilities.

The hardest group to move is often the veteran teachers who are not interested in change. All too frequently, they have always taught the way they themselves were taught, which was usually teacher-driven lessons. Converting veteran teachers to a more-student-talk model requires as much time, if not more, as the principal would spend with a novice teacher. As in many scenarios with the veteran teacher group, the principal had better come prepared to defend why increasing student talk is beneficial and how it would benefit the teachers' instruction.

Up to this point, this chapter has focused on the principal's role as the instructional leader and how to navigate that role, but how do we distinguish an instructional leader from anyone else in the building? It is a term used freely and often by administrators and those aspiring to "be in the chair." The difficult part in defining this term is that there is not a black-and-white, clear-cut answer. It is rather a murky mixture of instructional knowledge, an aptitude for leadership, logistical prowess, relational ability, and sometimes an undefined "it" factor. So, how do we identify these people?

As our motivation, we also need to realize the implication of being wrong in hiring poor instructional leaders. I have spent a significant amount of time going over the many roles of the principal. None of those roles is more important than the instructional leadership responsibilities, but they all work in concert with one another to create a successful campus. If we are placing poor instructional leaders on our campuses, then we are forfeiting any opportunities for teacher growth and thereby directly affecting student achievement.

Just as chapter 1 discusses what instructional leaders need to look for in a teacher, this chapter examines what we should look for in a principal to ensure that we are hiring someone capable of filling the role of the instructional leader. The first step in that process is establishing what our criteria are for an instructional leader. What is it that we are going to expect an instructional leader to be able to do? Based on what I have discussed to this point, what non-negotiables are we going to set?

In searching for instructional leaders to lead a campus, those making the ultimate decisions must be able to sift through all of the debris of flashy educational jargon used by those pursuing instructional leadership positions. Words like *engagement*, *differentiation*, or any other handful of terms are readily thrown around by principal applicants in an attempt to demonstrate a superior knowledge of instruction. Talk is cheap in this endeavor.

It seems as though principal applicants feel that merely being able to use flashy terms correctly in a conversation will get them a job. To be honest, sometimes it works. If this were enough, though, why are so many schools lacking instructional leadership? Why is it not enough to have a conversational knowledge of terms that are important to quality instruction?

So, what is it we are truly looking for? Do we not want instructional leaders to be able to have an understanding of this flashy educational jargon? These terms are frequently thrown about but are nonetheless undeniably important to quality instruction. What we want to identify is how those seeking instructional leadership positions can implement this terminology in a workable instructional program. We need to see that they can go past conversational knowledge of these concepts and demonstrate a working understanding of the terms and concepts in a campus or classroom setting.

The problem is that the skills we require of educators to be successful are somewhat abstract in nature. In education, we do not have an easy way to measure effectiveness, like referring to past sales quotas or production numbers, when making decisions on whom to hire. That is the blessing and curse of education. One cannot measure instructional efficiency, teacher effectiveness, or student achievement by quotas or production numbers. Our profession is different. Our profession has a human factor that is hard to define or measure, unlike other professions.

So, what is the answer to measuring instructional capacity in leadership? As stated earlier, it requires examining our current determination practices and identifying the assumptions we make that lead to poor decisions on leadership. We must first identify the areas that provide us the false data that then leads to misguided decisions. Without being reflective in our practices, we are dooming ourselves to continue to make the same mistakes.

One of the false assumptions we make in looking for capable principals is that one can only be an instructional leader in one's content area. When staffing campuses, we set teachers and students up to fail if we give into this mind-set. Principals should not be chosen solely because they have a content background in an area of weakness on the intended campus. On the surface, it seems like a good idea, but what happens the next year if the campus's weaknesses are in another content area? Do we at that point go out and find a different principal?

Consider what the value would be in a principal who could only evaluate instruction in one content area. Not only would incredible inefficiency ensue, but also the message that the principal is conveying to the staff would need to be considered. The message the staff receives can spiral in a couple different directions, none of which is positive. One result could be that teachers not in the principal's content area may feel devalued. Alternatively, the staff could feel that the principal is incompetent.

It would be naïve to think that principals can be content experts in every subject in their building. With that said, the type of instructional leadership that principals should provide should transcend content areas. Sound instructional practices are not necessarily math or reading strategies; they are just quality instructional strategies applicable to all content areas. It is imperative that a principal as an instructional leader feel confident in any content area, observing instruction for what it is.

Once again, this sense of instructional confidence is critical. The principal, when implementing instructional change, will inevitably be challenged at some point by teachers who may believe their content knowledge is superior, therefore trumping the instructional initiative of the principal. A strong instructional leader is able to convey the importance and value of the practice and its ability to transcend content. By being able to stand up to challenges, principals can cement their role as instructional leaders, thereby galvanizing their initiatives with the staff instead of allowing them to be viewed as optional practices.

In continuing to work through some of the false assumptions we make that can prevent us from identifying quality instructional leaders, let us discuss one of the false assumptions we make right out of the gate when we interview candidates. Candidates typically woo their way through interviews by waxing poetic and using all the mind-numbing instructional gibberish mentioned earlier. This is because, to be honest, they have the playbook: Everyone asks the same questions or variations thereof. Candidates know going into the interview that they are expected to talk the talk of instructional leadership.

Over time, decision makers have really struggled to figure out a way to have candidates demonstrate whether they can walk the walk of instructional leadership. In the first chapter, I discuss job-embedded interviews for teachers. Creating a similar process for administrators is equally necessary but not nearly as easy. Creating job-embedded activities to gauge such abstract skills as leadership is simply difficult. By beginning to think outside the box, there are definitely places we can start.

To start, it is strongly recommended that decision makers put some data in front of candidates during principal interviews. Through this data, candidates could work through certain scenarios and situations that the decision makers have created. In this way, decision makers could determine if candidates handle the situations in ways that display their instructional leadership capacity. It is important to put the candidates for these instructional leadership positions in as many applicable situations as possible.

Since these are important decisions on campus leadership, district administrators had better choose principals who know their way around data. For instance, decision makers should find out if candidates can identify areas of need from assessment data. Can they pinpoint weak learning standards? Also, decision makers need to see if candidates have the ability to develop a plan for remediation that will identify students who need additional instruction. Can they analyze data and find out which students need what?

Another false assumption often made is that all principal candidates were good teachers because they decided to apply to be a principal, which is essentially the master teacher for a campus. In the interview process, a substantial part should be dedicated to evaluating ability as a teacher. Can candidates demonstrate that they are a quality teacher? Remember, the person hired to be the principal is going to be the lead teacher for the campus. Accordingly, principals had better be able to hold their own in a classroom.

The key word in interviews is *demonstrate*. If you are the decision maker, understand that there is nothing wrong with asking the candidates to prepare a lesson in their content area to present during the interview. Principal candidates should be able to knock your socks off walking you through a lesson cycle, floor you by describing how they use formative assessment to make instructional decisions, and wow you by discussing their ability to collect and analyze data to improve student achievement. Then, and only then, if they can prove themselves capable of being a master teacher, should they move forward in the interview process.

It would be at this stage of the process that one could determine whether a candidate has what may be termed *general* or *conversational* knowledge of instruction as opposed to the preferred application level of instructional knowledge. As discussed earlier, a conversational level of instructional knowledge is not enough for someone to be the master teacher of the campus. The principal as the instructional leader should be like a doctor: the principal should use instructional knowledge to diagnose instructional weaknesses and then come up with the prescription to fix any problems.

Placing principals on campuses who cannot *walk the walk* instructionally is basically educational malpractice. The instructional responsibilities of the principal are too important to forego in lieu of anything else. Principals are placed on campuses to be the *master teacher*, the *instructional leaders*. If we know this to be true and we profess that is what our intentions are, then how can we have it any other way? At the end of the day, if we are not hiring principals to fit this requirement, we are willingly allowing students to suffer.

SUMMARY

As the principal of a campus, your role as an instructional leader is the most important you will ever have. Accepting this role is acknowledging the many responsibilities that encompass being an instructional leader. In this role, you are not only responsible for setting the instructional program in motion for the campus, but you are also responsible for those implementing the instructional program. Just as the teachers are responsible for meeting the students where they are academically and growing them over the course of the school year, you are responsible for the same with your teachers. The job does not end once you hire them. Not understanding or being able to carry out these responsibilities can ultimately lead to the failure of the campus.

THREE POINTS TO REMEMBER

1. The principal is the master teacher of the campus.
2. The principal must make instruction a clear priority on campus.
3. The principal is responsible for the instructional program.

Chapter Three

Formative Assessment

*The Truest Evaluator of Quality
When Evaluating Lessons*

This chapter goes right out on the proverbial limb with the declaration that formative assessment should be the bedrock of any instructional plan. When discussing strategies that highly impact and truly drive quality instruction, there is no better practice than the effective use of formative assessments. When used properly and efficiently, formative assessment allows teachers to know where each student is in their learning, provides the means for reflective practices of lesson effectiveness, and gives the ultimate guidance on pacing.

    That being said, have you ever run across a situation where your and someone else's definitions of something are totally different? Imagine that you are at a conference discussing a fundamental practice of your job, and then you hear a coworker next to you say, "Yeah, I do it like that, too." At that point, you realize your coworker does not have a clue about that particular practice because you have seen that person at work and know what he brings to the table.

    Sometimes educators are like that with formative assessment. You may be having a conversation or attending a presentation, and you hear that one teacher say, "Yeah, I do that." In shock, you do a double take. Then you begin to wonder what that teacher believes formative assessment is because you know that what you have seen in that teacher's classroom is definitely not it. Many teachers define *formative assessment* differently and apply it differently in their classrooms.

Why is it that one of the most basic practices in education is so widely misunderstood? Principals may have teachers on their campus who believe they are accomplishing formative assessment through weekly quizzes. Other teachers believe their unit tests are their formative assessment of student learning. Some teachers cringe at the idea of being required to assess students daily because that would require way too much work. Other teachers believe that they do formative assessment daily, as they measure student learning by how many hands go up when they ask questions.

For all intents and purposes, these teachers are not necessarily wrong. All of the aforementioned assessment strategies contain elements of formative assessment. The issue is that these strategies are ridiculously inefficient in achieving the goal of formative assessment. This chapter's objective is to outline daily formative-assessment practices that impact student achievement and work to increase the quality of instruction in our classrooms.

To accomplish this objective, I not only discuss the role of formative assessment in the classroom but also work through examples and the rationales behind their effective use to increase student achievement. I go into great detail on the principal's role in teaching, observing, and coaching teachers in using formative assessment in their classrooms to guide their instruction. Finally, I outline what the principal should be looking for to ensure that formative-assessment practices are being used efficiently and effectively.

Before principals can discuss formative-assessment practices with their staffs, they need to make sure their staffs understand the difference between formative and summative assessment. There is a big distinction to be made here. Teachers need to understand that formative assessments guide instruction and are intended to measure the learning process. In contrast, summative assessments measure what students have learned at the conclusion of the learning process. The distinction between the two is important when evaluating students, teachers, and the instructional program of the campus.

To convey to a staff the powerful impact formative assessment can have on instruction, principals need to have a solid understanding of what it is, which one would assume to be a prerequisite for a principal. In addition, principals should know how to implement formative assessment across any classroom. For principals, the knowledge of and ability to apply formative assessment goes much further than a simple textbook definition.

To fully grasp the higher-level understanding of formative assessment required of principals as instructional leaders, they must acknowledge the relationship between rigor and formative assessment. This means that, in order to understand formative assessment, the principal must also have a working understanding of rigor. Later in the chapter, you will realize that rigor is essential to quality formative-assessment practices.

So at this point, let's examine guidelines and non-negotiables for both formative assessment and rigor as I work out the relationship between the two. I start by discussing the four guidelines of formative assessment. I use these guidelines as a reference point for my discussions on formative assessment, and then I explore each one individually. The guidelines are:

- formative assessment should be a daily part of instruction;
- formative assessment should be intentional;
- formative assessment can be informal; and
- formative assessment should be used to guide instruction.

In addressing the first guideline, principals should set the expectation that formative assessments should be a daily practice in classrooms across a campus. As I later discuss at length, the only way to know how students are performing is for teachers to make sure they are checking for understanding. If teachers are not checking for understanding daily, they have no way of knowing who has it and who does not. Without daily formative assessment, the teachers have no real data to inform them about when to move forward in the curriculum.

The second guideline is that formative assessment should be intentional. Formative assessment is not a run-of-the-mill activity. Throughout this chapter, I discuss formative assessment with a planned and intentional purpose. Being intentional with formative-assessment practices requires teachers to think with the end in mind. In other words, teachers must know both where the students need to be and what level of rigor they will need to be at. Teachers will then need to use this knowledge to create formative assessments that adequately prepare their students for success on a summative exam.

A common misconception of formative assessment is that it is a formal activity that must result in a grade. This view of formative assessments could not be further from the truth. In fact, not only is the misconception a farce, but it also represents a poor understanding of the practice. Formative assessment can and should happen multiple times a day. Formative assessment can range from something as simple as a thumbs-up to the ever-popular exit ticket and everything in between. Formative assessment is designed to measure the learning process, not the learning end product.

Finally, formative assessment should be used to guide instruction. Unfortunately, all too often, teachers are consumed with covering material, looking at curriculum calendars, or finding opportunities to fit in pet assignments. However, the only thing teachers should be using to determine whether they should move forward through the curriculum is the students' progress in learning the required standards. As educators, we should allow the students to tell us when they are ready to move on.

Indeed, knowing when to speed up or slow down through the curriculum should be dictated by the students' comprehension of the presented material, not the curriculum calendar or some other reason. Students show us they are ready to move forward in the curriculum by how much and how well they have learned. In turn, the only way to gauge students' progress in learning the required standards is through a check for understanding, otherwise known as formative assessment.

Now that I have established the guidelines for formative assessment, let us discuss rigor. *Rigor* may be the most used and least understood word in education. As educators, we know rigor is important. As administrators, we know rigor is something we are supposed to look for in our teachers' classrooms, but we have a hard time identifying it. Teachers and administrators both spend inordinate amounts of time in professional-development workshops about rigor. Yet very seldom can two educators provide the same definition or even expectations for the specificity of rigor.

How, then, do principals develop a common language on their campuses to define *rigor*? After all, *rigor* is a term that is freely used by so many educators, yet nearly everyone has their own spin on it. For example, some would say it is defined by additional schoolwork and others say by more difficult work. There are some who would say that rigor is the difference between a standard curriculum and an advanced curriculum. Still others believe rigor is in the abstract and achieved through outside-the-box lesson designs and projects.

In chapter 1, I discuss hiring a principal to be the master teacher of the campus. In placing principals, it is imperative that these master teachers be confident in their understanding of rigor. Not only do they need to be confident in their understanding of rigor, but their understanding must also closely match the school's understanding. This requires clearly defined expectations for rigor throughout the learning organization.

It is also crucial that this organizational expectation for rigor is one that can easily be communicated and one that everyone in the organization, from administrators to teachers, can be clearly on the same page about. To accomplish this, everyone in must speak the same language. Continuing to talk about rigor without a common expectation is another way we set campuses and principals up to fail.

For the purpose of common language, *rigor* is the depth of knowledge a student needs to have to successfully demonstrate mastery of a learning standard. In this working core definition, I remove the logistics of rigor. Too often, we get caught up in trying to give a tangible description of rigor. At this point, we are not going to worry about lesson design, activities, or questions. All we want to look at it is the learning standard and the depth to which we are asked to teach it. We frequently make the idea of rigor entirely more complicated than it needs to be.

When working with this definition, principals may need to explain to their teachers the difference between determining the depth to which something is taught using their own interests or biases on a standard versus using the actual standard that dictates the depth of understanding required. No matter where one teaches across the nation, every state and learning organization has learning standards, and the level of rigor is clearly defined in the learning standards. As the instructional leaders on our campuses, we must be able to convey this first indicator of rigor and thereby begin to eliminate rigor based on personal preference.

An example of teachers determining depth using personal interest or biases is evident in "pet lessons," or those lessons teachers love to teach every year but that tend to take more time than is dictated by the scope and sequence. Pet lessons can also be enjoyable for the kids but do not expose the students to the required level of rigor to meet the learning standard. Coincidentally, these are the lessons teachers will fight tooth and nail to keep, resulting in the need for the principal as the instructional leader to step in to explain lesson expectations.

The principal as coach should discuss how the learning standards drive the scope and sequence, not our opinions. The teacher should not be making "I think . . . I feel" decisions. The principal should explain how the pet lesson prevented the teacher from teaching to the appropriate rigor, and it also caused the teacher to be unable to ensure that there was adequate time to teach all the other learning standards to their appropriate levels of rigor. During this meeting, the principal could also work with the teacher to find ways to integrate parts of the lesson into the appropriate time allotted.

Now that I have established guidelines for both formative assessment and rigor, the next step is to focus on the application of the two and begin to see how formative assessment and rigor work in concert with one another. Instructional leaders and teachers need a well-thought-out plan for rigor because ultimately rigorous instruction cannot be achieved off the cuff. That said, planning for rigor in our lessons is not so difficult that it requires late nights and eighty-hour workweeks.

As a matter of fact, rigor can most easily be added to any lesson through thoughtful and intentional questioning practices, which is a basic form of formative assessment. If we train our teachers to ask the right questions and encourage a shift in focus to what our expectations are for student responses, rigor is easily attained while still respecting teaching styles and teacher autonomy in the classroom. Of course, like many tasks, this questioning skill is easier said than done.

We ask questions all the time in our daily interactions. Asking questions seems to be one of those teaching skills that a person off the street could have without spending one day in the classroom. To some degree this is true, in the sense of simply posing a question. It takes practically no skill at all to ask leading or no-brainer questions. However, the skill of planning one's questions is in maximizing the effectiveness of the questions to truly guide instruction. This stipulation makes the task exponentially more difficult.

The practice of questioning is one of the most underrated practices in education. Indeed, questioning students may be one of the most effective and basic yet most overlooked forms of formative assessment. When students are able to answer questions regarding material that is at a high level of rigor, in which they had to apply the intended information from the learning standard being taught, one can safely assume that students have demonstrated that they have learned something. This questioning practice does not require a pen or paper, nor does it cost a day of instruction to implement. All that is needed is some planning at the front end.

Sounds pretty easy, right? There is no need for bells and whistles in formative assessment, just good old-fashioned questioning practices. This practice does not require dog and pony shows or elaborate activities. Teachers just need knowledge of the learning standards and an understanding of the depth at which students need to grasp them. The real work comes in the preparation of the questions, the practices involved in the delivery, and the knowledge of what to do with the students' answers, right or wrong.

However, a frequent misconception about the practice of questioning is that teachers can do it without any prior preparation. Teachers who are expert questioners are those who put in a significant amount of time at the front end of instruction planning for quality questioning. As a side note, working with teachers to convince them of the benefits of this type of questioning practice may be a large task in of itself for the principal, as it may be a major paradigm shift for some.

One should be aware that there are several common mistakes to discuss with questioning. The assumed simplicity of asking a question lures teachers into believing questioning to be a run-of-the-mill task. When really taking time to analyze the goals and intended outcomes from quality targeted questioning, it is easy to see that questioning may be the hardest thing teachers do in everyday instruction, yet it may receive the least amount of attention.

Why is quality questioning so difficult to accomplish? The answer, in part, is that there is an inordinate amount of planning that needs to be dedicated to the questions themselves and then the additional planning of to whom to ask the questions. In fact, planning for quality questioning is a multistep process. In order to achieve the desired results, one has to have a deep understanding of the curriculum, the level of rigor each student will be expected to reach to demonstrate mastery, and also the daily level of understanding of each student in the classroom.

Being a multistep process, planning for quality questioning requires the teacher to first formulate appropriate-level questions that reflect how students will be assessed. Then the teacher must also anticipate the student responses and determine which answers are acceptable. Yes, teachers must identify what they need to hear in the student responses prior to asking the questions. In order to plan accordingly, teachers must be aware of how the information is going to be assessed and to what level of rigor students will be held accountable.

Having an understanding of solid questioning practices allows the teacher to have the baseline for creating and shaping the questions they ask in class. Certainly, all educators understand that high-stakes summative assessments seldom ask simple computation questions, yet asking low-level questions is a common practice in many classrooms. For example, a teacher who is teaching single-digit addition might only ask students simple computation questions: 1 plus 2, 3 plus 4, and so on. This practice of asking lower-level questions is usually borne of teachers' fear of losing time.

The problem with simple computational problems is that students will be later asked multistep questions on summative assessments that require them to break down and analyze word problems. One does not have to be a rocket scientist to predict that these students will not be successful on a high-stakes exam that asks them to extrapolate numbers from a word problem through the type of instruction discussed here. Instructional leaders cannot allow such disconnects between instruction and assessments.

Truly, principals cannot expect teachers to adequately prepare students by teaching at one level and assessing at another. Teachers have to teach students the way they are going to be assessed on summative and high-stakes exams. This means the instructional leader must understand how well the teaching matches the assessment before approaching teachers to set expectations. The principal as the instructional leader must be able to lead teachers in creating opportunities in their daily instruction that makes students comfortable and familiar in summative and high-stakes settings.

The first step in planning for questioning is understanding what the end game is. Once again, we need a "begin with the end in mind" mind-set. A teacher must know exactly how far the students are to go in the content for them to be successful on a summative assessment. This requires a strong scope and sequence that outlines both content and rigor. Once the teacher understands the end game, she can establish the length of time the content standard requires and determine the level of rigor the students must be able to demonstrate. At that point, she can begin the process of formulating appropriate questions to assess the progress.

So, once teachers understand the necessary rigor of the content standard and the amount of time required thereof, they then should formulate the questions they will ask. For reference purposes, I go back to the *essential questions* mentioned in the first chapter. By no means should these essential questions be the only questions the teacher will ask, but they will be the preformulated questions that evaluate student learning for each day. The responses from these essential questions will be the deciding factor for the teacher about whether the class is ready to move on or whether they need additional time with the content.

When evaluating the practice, the principal must determine if the time spent on the topic and the level of rigor are appropriately matched. It is only through this appropriate balance that the teacher and the instructional leader can accurately assess student learning. For instance, for a content standard that requires five days in the scope and sequence, the rigor of the day 1 questions will be much lower than that of the day 5 questions.

The important takeaway here is to scaffold the level of rigor in the questioning as the time in the content progresses. Make sure that the teachers are also being mindful of the vocabulary used through the progression of the content. By the end of the time predetermined by the scope and sequence, teachers should have strong formative data informing them whether students know the material at levels that ensure their success on any summative assessment that is to follow.

Conversely, if the data says the opposite, the students require some sort of remediation, and the instructional leader may see a need to evaluate the curriculum and instruction. In this evaluation, the teacher, with guidance from the principal, should be looking at missed opportunities, the level of rigor provided in the learning standards, and the materials and delivery of the lesson or lessons used to provide the instruction.

The second part of quality questioning involves planning not only whom to ask the questions of but also, as discussed earlier, mapping the intended student responses. This step in quality questioning is often an afterthought for teachers. Traditionally, teachers ask questions, students raise their hands to answer, and the teachers choose someone to answer the question. This is an age-old practice whose roots are probably in the first one-room schoolhouse.

The practice of only calling on students with their hands raised could be one of the most detrimental practices still being implemented in our classrooms, and it just happens to be one of the most traditional practices on every campus across the country. The reason this practice is so detrimental to student learning and achievement is that it allows students to opt out of instruction. Not only does it *allow* a student to opt out of instruction, but one also could argue that it *encourages* students to opt out of instruction.

This practice sends the message to students that, if they do not want to participate, they do not have to as long they choose not to raise their hands. To top it all off, the teacher will be completely fine with it. Teachers will chase homework until they are blue in the face, but if you do not want to participate in class, no big deal. Now this is obviously sarcasm, but the practice is real and routinely occurs on almost every, if not every, campus across the nation.

This discussion of how teachers choose the students to call on is the perfect time to bring up the practice of targeted questioning. Targeted questioning simply means having a very specific plan for whom the teacher wants to hear from in the classroom. Choosing students through prior formative-assessment data allows teachers to target whom they get their responses from, as opposed to leaving it to chance. This practice eliminates the opt-out culture that teachers promote through poor questioning practices.

Targeted questioning ensures that reluctant learners participate throughout the lesson cycle. Not only are reluctant learners the beneficiaries of this practice, but all students, even the brightest in the class, can benefit when they inevitably run into bumps in their learning journeys. This practice allows teachers the powerful, proactive opportunity to address learning gaps in the moment, based on formative-assessment data, as opposed to being reactionary, waiting for struggles on a summative assessment, when it is too late to address instructional needs.

Teachers can replace antiquated hand-raising practices by implementing a targeted-questioning strategy referred to as a *no-hands policy*. This policy eliminates any opportunity for students to opt out of instruction. A no-hands policy is the first step in planning for whom we call on in our classrooms. The initial implementation of this practice takes time and requires dedication by the entire campus but yields impressive results by creating an environment where every student is held accountable for learning.

Teachers implementing a no-hands policy have an increased responsibility to be prepared for questioning in the classroom. They now shift their focus from randomly calling on students to planning based on the need to hear from particular students, as dictated by data from formative assessments. By not calling on students with their hands raised, with the goal of hearing the correct answer, the teacher may gain greater information from hearing an incorrect answer.

The coaching point to look for in implementing a targeted-questioning practice, such as a no-hands policy or one like it, is to stress the difference between targeted and random questioning. Teachers may believe they are practicing targeted questioning when they draw popsicle sticks with students' names on them or when they draw numbers correlated to names in the grade book when choosing whom to call on. These practices are anything but targeted and are completely random. These random practices take the control away from the teachers.

By incorporating a targeted-questioning practice, such as a no-hands policy, the teacher forces the issue of hearing from the students he needs to hear from the most. Every classroom teacher in America knows the kids they can rely on for correct answers and, in turn, knows the students who struggle to have the right answers. Whom should the teacher be hearing from the most in the class? It is the student who struggles. The more information teachers can gather from this group of students, the more teachers can clarify during instruction to increase students' ability to learn the intended content.

The next step in the questioning process, one that is often forgotten, is preparing for student responses. This step also significantly adds to both the difficulty and effort of the overall task. Too often in classrooms, teachers ask excellent questions but let students off the hook by allowing lower-level answers in return. If you have ever been in the classroom, you are probably guilty of this yourself. In doing this, we are allowing students to get away with "close enough." The establishment of a "close enough" culture is almost as detrimental as the opt-out culture discussed earlier.

The creation of a "close enough" culture undermines our instructional efforts. By rushing though our questioning, settling for low-level student responses, we hamstring the practice. We also limit our students and establish the expectation that getting "close enough" is acceptable. This mind-set leads teachers to ultimate failure in their goal of preparing students for success, as "close enough" is not going to take them where they need to be on the high-stakes summative assessments that ultimately judge their academic readiness.

In preparing for student responses, teachers may actually write out the desired responses to their questions. The plan for what they need to hear from students ensures that the students will reach the targeted standard on the summative assessment. Teachers plan for such things as the vocabulary they expect, the sequencing of a response, and the overall amount of information required. This step helps teachers find the holes in their own instruction, understand where students need prompting, and have data to make decisions on when to move forward in the curriculum.

This process takes questioning to a much higher instructional level than the traditional two-step process of teachers asking questions and students answering them. In planning the questions to match the required rigor of the standard, the teacher is ensuring that students are prepared for the rigor expected of them. In presenting questions in formats that the students will find on the summative assessment, the teacher is ensuring that they are prepared. In anticipating appropriate student responses, the teacher is both establishing the learning expectation and planning for students to meet those expectations.

Without implementing these steps in preparing for questioning, teachers might as well be blindfolded and throwing darts at a dartboard. Asking questions off the cuff leads to missing rigor expectations. Not anticipating student responses is minimizing learning expectations because the teacher has not identified what the expectation is for themselves. The practice becomes so watered down without preparation that it essentially becomes a low-level cognitive activity that wastes valuable instructional time, which I have already established we are in a vicious fight for.

After the planning process comes the means of delivery for our targeted-questioning practices. The ability to plan for student involvement is one of the most positive characteristics of targeted questioning. When there is a plan for targeted questioning, the number of students who participate skyrockets. By increasing the number of students answering questions, teachers increase the amount of formative data from their students.

For example, traditionally a teacher asks a question and calls on one student to answer. If the student answers incorrectly, the teacher corrects him. If the student is correct, the teacher moves on. What would happen if we were to get a much greater number of students involved in each question, simply by modifying how we pose our questions?

One strategy to achieve increased student participation through questioning is *agree/disagree* questions. In posing questions this way, you drastically increase the number of students participating while also practicing targeted-questioning strategies. The one thing required of the teacher is to transition from presenter to facilitator. The following are two examples, one math and one reading, of what this practice might look like in the classroom:

Math Teacher: Who can come up and set up the first step to solve this equation?

Struggling Student Johnny: (He works the first step on the board.)

Math Teacher: Who agrees with what Johnny put as the first step to solve this equation?

High-Level Sally: I do not agree because Johnny did not flip the sign when he crossed the equal sign.

Math Teacher: Do you agree with what Sally is saying?

The conversation continues as the teacher works each step of the problem.

Reading Teacher: Who can summarize the passage we just read?

Struggling Student Jim: (Jim gives an acceptable summary.)

Reading Teacher: Jennifer, do you agree with Jim's summary?

Struggling Student Jennifer: Yes.

Reading Teacher: Why do you agree?

Struggling Student Jennifer: (Jennifer explains her rationale.)

Reading Teacher: (High-Achieving) Bill, can you show me the text evidence to support this summary?

The instructional leader must emphasize two points while training teachers in this process. First, randomness is not the key. The goal is increased participation but not randomly increased participation. As mentioned in the discussion of targeted questioning, teachers should plan whom to question. With this strategy, however, teachers need to have a plan for both the struggle to answer and the explanation of the answer. The process does not stop with a student answering incorrectly.

Earlier I discussed the teacher who only called on the students with their hands up and how that was not a good practice. Through the strategy referenced here, the teacher is able to make use of the kids who always have the right answers but without allowing them to dominate the conversation during the lesson. The high-achieving students in the classroom now take the traditional role of the teacher as the one who determines if an answer to a question is right or wrong. Notice, though, that the students are not just allowed to say "yes" or "I agree" but must provide their rationale for why an answer is correct or incorrect.

The second point of emphasis is ensuring that you are hearing from your struggling students. The key here is forcing them to voice their struggles. It is not enough for the teacher to hear the wrong answer; he needs to hear or see where the breakdown is. By requiring students to talk through their struggles, explaining their rationale, the teacher is able to address gaps in student learning. Look how much additional information a teacher is able to gain versus a traditional questioning strategy, where teachers simply look for "yes" or "no" or right or wrong.

By having a plan for questioning, a teacher goes into the lesson knowing exactly whom they want to hear from, with the intention of gaining knowledge of student progress. Sometimes this may lead to feedback that does not positively reflect on a lesson but gives very positive information for moving forward. For instance, can the lesson be deemed successful if only the top 10 percent of the students in the class can correctly answer what we have deemed essential questions, whose sole purpose is to gauge student learning?

Teachers can make their lessons look amazing all day long by calling on the right kids and getting all the right responses, but who wins in that situation? Is it not more valuable to know a lesson did not work as we thought, but at the end of the day, we leave knowing what needs to be done the next day to really bring it home and make sure every kid learned the content objective? Targeting questioning is what makes that possible.

That leads to how we gather and use the information gained from targeted questioning to really guide our instruction. As the instructional leader, principals need to determine what benchmark percentage the campus will establish to move forward in the curriculum with formative assessments. A common benchmark percentage that may be an appropriate starting point is 80 percent. This means that, in a class of twenty students, sixteen students would need to demonstrate that they were able to answer the essential question for the day to move the class forward the following day.

How to gather the data from targeted questioning involves so much more than simply looking at what students answered correctly or incorrectly. Once a teacher is comfortable in targeted-questioning practices, she will see that one of the greatest sources of student data comes from how students react to the questions:

- What prior knowledge do students draw from to answer questions?
- What vocabulary are the students using?
- Where are students stumbling?
- What are the common misunderstandings?

A great coaching point is to have teachers document the student reactions to the questions throughout the day, especially secondary teachers, who may be teaching the same class six times a day.

Teachers can track this important information from class to class in order to respond to and tweak instruction to increase the effectiveness of their targeted questioning. Tracking where students struggle and have common misconceptions, mistakes, and misunderstandings helps the teacher critique lessons while allowing her to manage instruction during the lesson. This creates an environment of constant instructional flexibility and efficiency. Maximizing the time we have with our students is essential in education when students are busier outside of school than ever before.

The other key in formative-assessment data is discerning static formative-assessment data from real-time formative-assessment data. One of the most common responses from teachers to the question of how someone uses formative assessment to guide instruction is the use of exit tickets or variations thereof. Exit tickets have made it to the top of the list in educator lingo, the new hot fad, like acid-washed jeans back in the day, but as popular as they have become, are they the most effective formative tool teachers should be using?

The issue with using static formative assessments like exit tickets and the dreaded "quiz" is that the information teachers collect is too old to really make any formative use of it. Yes, exit tickets and quizzes provide us information about student learning, but teachers are not able to evaluate this information until the students have left the class and instruction is completed for the day.

Assessment data of this nature does not directly impact student learning until the next time we see students. The issue this presents is that, by the next day's instruction, teachers are more likely moving on to the next step or stage of the content. The student will be expected to be able to apply the day's prior knowledge, therefore resulting in the student falling further behind. By changing our practices to incorporate more real-time formative-assessment data, we can actually adjust our instruction to the students' learning needs during the course of the lesson cycle.

When using real-time formative assessments, teachers are tailoring instruction to the needs of their students during the lesson cycle. This practice allows the teacher to make instructional adjustments on the fly based on student needs. Teaching from a lesson plan, without real-time formative assessment, keeps teachers in their safe place, where they are in control from start to finish; however, students may get left behind in the pursuit to maintain control.

The fear and reality is that incorporating real-time formative assessments likely will derail the lesson plan, but it allows the teacher to clarify misunderstandings on the front end, taking a more proactive approach to instruction. This proactive approach allows teachers to keep more students on track for success on our summative assessments. This is in direct contrast to the traditional model, where teachers are reactionary and try to clarify misunderstandings in a remedial setting after the summative-assessment results come in.

The difference between static formative assessments and real-time formative assessments can be illustrated in the following narrative. Let's say two people go to the hospital with the same problem. One sees a doctor who immediately diagnoses the problem and treats the patient, and the patient survives.

The other patient sees a different doctor. This doctor sits back and observes. However, this approach results in the patient dying. After the patient is dead, the doctor collects all the information and at that point is able to determine a diagnosis, albeit obviously too late to affect the outcome. Instructional leaders cannot allow teachers to fall into the mind-set of the second doctor and wait until students fail to determine what the problem was, when there is nothing we can do to help.

Changing the focus from traditional, static formative assessments to a real-time formative assessment, such as targeted questioning, allows the teacher to receive up-to-the-moment updates on his students' learning. Tracking the formative data you receive from targeted questioning may seem difficult initially. Traditionally, teachers are used to receiving data from a paper-and-pencil activity, where the data from targeted questioning may seem more abstract in nature. The benefit of real-time formative assessment is that it is conducted and assessed throughout the lesson cycle.

Another important data point of formative assessment, one that is usually an afterthought for educators, is how formative assessment drives the pacing of learning. Principals need to ask teachers how they determine when to move forward through a curriculum. Too often, principals might get a response involving a curriculum calendar, and to be honest, that should strike absolute fear in the hearts of principals everywhere. Scope and sequences are important tools for instruction but should be used as a suggested route, not the only route.

When traveling on vacation, if you come upon a traffic jam and you have an opportunity to either reroute or sit in traffic for two hours, which option are you going to choose? The sane among us will choose to reroute. To sit in traffic wasting vacation time when there is an alternative route that will take a fraction of the time getting us to our destination just does not make sense. Why, then, do we do that with our students? Formative assessment allows for all the reroutes.

For the sake of following a scope and sequence, teachers will forgo their better judgment to make sure they follow their calendars instead of using their own common sense. Using formative assessment to drive instruction is taking advantage of the reroutes. Using formative assessment correctly can both speed up and slow down instruction as the teacher deems necessary from students' demonstration of learning.

Teachers are perpetually afraid of running out of time. Trying to convince a teacher that it is okay to slow down is a much harder sell than many outside of education may believe. The key to selling this idea is that, if teachers use formative assessment properly, it may later be okay to speed up. In the end, getting through the curriculum on time should result.

Principals should keep in mind that, if a teacher constantly has to slow down due to their formative-assessment data, the instructional leader will have a pretty good sign they may have an instructional issue to address. Formative-assessment data that says teachers need to slow down is essentially telling them that their kids are not getting it. If a teacher always needs additional time, their formatives are communicating they are likely falling behind.

Another powerful yet underrated aspect of formative assessment is the opportunity it provides teachers to have direct reflection on their lessons. As educators, like everyone else, we are not perfect. The job the instructional leader has in front of her here is convincing teachers that formative assessment provides a great opportunity. As I discuss in greater depth in chapter 5, teachers judge themselves by their scores. Sometimes, teachers do not want to look at themselves in the mirror with poor results, but this is actually the most impactful time to do so.

Let's be honest: There are times principals observe lessons that are simply amazing and should be viewed by every teacher on campus, while at other times principals observe lessons that are created with every intent to be amazing, but they fall flat. Then there are the lessons that principals observe that do not seem to be going well but then the students somehow miraculously get it. How are principals supposed to communicate the difference between the varied outcomes? Formative assessment is the key to answering that question.

It is for this reason that it is important that the principal be able to communicate the power of formative assessment, to convey that information to their staffs, and to train their teachers in proper implementation. Formative assessments take on many different shapes and sizes. As with anything, some versions will work better in some areas than others. It is up to the principal to have the depth of knowledge to facilitate which forms work best within varied content and teaching styles.

As I move forward, it is important to dispel some myths and note some poor applications of formative assessment commonly exhibited under the guise of quality instructional practice. It is still shocking to hear through interviews and discussions how poorly educators, teachers, and principals alike understand formative assessment. What should be a foundational practice in every school, many educators seem not to have a clue about but, once again, can talk the talk.

The first formative-assessment application issue to discuss is the *exit ticket*. The issue is not the validity of the exit ticket as a formative assessment, but it is the reliance of this option as the increasingly popular go-to option for educators claiming to understand formative assessments. If principals really want to trip up applicants in an interview, ask them to describe how they intend to use formative assessment in their classroom without using exit tickets; then watch the awkward pondering as if you took away their top pitch. You take away the exit-ticket option, and many teachers seem lost without a second option.

As discussed earlier, it is not that exit tickets are not formative in nature; they have attributes of a formative assessment. The aspect to take issue with when evaluating the practice of exit tickets is the static data they produce. Exit tickets provide next-day feedback that does not affect instruction in the moment, thereby minimizing the practice's ultimate effectiveness.

A worse case is the teacher who does not even have that trick in the bag. This is the teacher who, when asked about formative assessment, can only refer to quizzes. Once again, it is not wrong to think that quizzes are formative in nature. The issue is that one would rather hear how a teacher uses formative assessment in a more immediate, daily manner. At the end of the day, the root purpose is to use formatives to drive instruction. Regular quizzes, unless specified, are usually given every couple days at most. This practice minimizes opportunities for instructional adjustments daily.

An inexcusable mistake commonly made regarding formative assessment is teachers' willingness to part with it. Too often, it seems that, when time is running short, the formative assessment is the first thing teachers feel they can scrap to keep the activity going. By all means, teachers must save the activity portion of the lesson, even if it means cutting the part that tells teachers if the activity was in any way effective in educating kids. Once again the sarcasm is obvious, but the rationale is real.

Administrators indirectly foster this environment. Administrators do not promote formative assessment with all the bells and whistles of flashy lessons. When was the last time a principal called teachers to a room to watch another teacher's formative-assessment practices? Or, here is an even better one, when was the last time a teacher called a principal into their room to see their formative assessment?

This is even reflected in professional-development opportunities provided throughout the year, where formative assessment plays second fiddle to topics like student engagement, group-work dynamics, and other more ballyhooed topics. For whatever reason, formative assessment does not have the flair of some of the more trendy topics in education, but there is not a more important topic in education.

While these other topics are important aspects of effective instruction, formative assessment is what ultimately gauges the effectiveness of those practices. To further illustrate this point, if you are running a race, consider formative assessment as the stopwatch. You can have a teacher create the flashiest lesson in the history of education, but without formative assessment to judge if the students learned anything, it is just that—a flashy lesson.

Principals in the role of instructional leaders cannot promote a learning environment where instructional leaders' flash is valued above formative assessment. The flash of activities in a lesson cannot be deemed successful, unless you are able to check for and measure student understanding. If students are unable to demonstrate their knowledge of the learning standard, the flash is all for naught.

An excellent example of flash over substance, and parts with formative assessment in one combined setting, is the very trendy practice of group work. As discussed in chapter 2, in preparing students for twenty-first-century jobs, some yet to be imagined, group dynamics have been said to be a skill our students need to be trained in. In trying to accomplish this, teachers often take the lazy approach of placing students in a group to work "cooperatively" but fail to check for understanding after the activity is complete, thereby wasting instructional time that they cannot afford to waste.

Think back fondly to your own school days, and you will likely fall into one of two groups when it comes to group work: the person who did all the work or the person who let the smart kid get you the good grade. Group work can be a positive practice regardless of which side of the fence you fall on, but unless there is an assessment at the conclusion of the activity, the teacher has no idea of each group member's knowledge of the intended material.

After discussing at length shifts in thinking for teachers (switching from a static formative-assessment approach to a more real-time targeted-questioning formative-assessment model), we turn to principals shifting their thinking in terms of expectations from lesson plans. This will require a major paradigm shift in what really is an archaic campus practice. In order to discuss how formative-assessment practices can take the place of traditional lesson plans, first it is important to ask ourselves, what is the true purpose of lesson plans?

The basic rationale for lesson plans is so that principals, as the leaders of instruction, can ensure that teachers have a plan for instruction that matches scope and sequence and uses the appropriate curriculum. This practice was established long before principals were viewed as instructional leaders. The practice of making lesson plans was initially instituted when principals were viewed more as managers.

Today it should be argued that principals, as instructional leaders, should not need lesson plans to accomplish this goal. Principals working as instructional leaders through quality observation and walk-through practices should have no issue ensuring that teachers stay on track. Using quality observation and walk-through practices, it is easy to evaluate whether a teacher is in the appropriate place in the curriculum.

A more consequential, student-driven practice than having general lesson plans turned in weekly would be having formative-assessment questions, or essential questions, being turned in weekly. This information would be important because the principal could see the level of rigor the teacher is assessing students on daily, with the additional benefit of seeing pacing. If the principal is satisfied with the level of rigor, the lesson evaluation comes in the question data. Essentially, if teachers are asking higher-level, rigorous questions and students are successful in answering the questions, why would principals care how the teacher got them there?

Another positive aspect of using formative assessment over traditional lesson plans is pacing. When used correctly, a teacher can rely on her formative-assessment practices to know when to move forward in the content or to slow down and reteach. The students' ability to answer essential questions, due to the level of rigor planned, allows the teacher to feel confident in deciding pacing. The reason this model is so much more beneficial than the traditional lesson-plan model is that a calendar is not dictating pace; student learning is.

At this point, it is probably necessary to dispel the "teaching to the test" argument, with all the talk of matching our questions to the formats students may see on a summative exam. How many jobs require certification exams? You likely had to take one to become an educator. These exams are commonplace in almost any profession our students will be seeking after their time with us.

Was it not your expectation that your program prepared you to be successful on that exam? Of course it was! It was expected that we were taught the information and to know how we would be expected to demonstrate that knowledge. If that was our expectation for the programs we took, should we not hold campus teachers accountable to the same expectations? These high-stakes summative assessments, whether you are for or against them, are how our students are weighed and measured. Principals need to that ensure teachers are providing a rich educational experience that will also ensure student success on these summative assessments.

There is a very distinct difference between teaching to a test and teaching to a level of rigor. Teaching to a test requires teachers to almost leak information. It innately implies cheating or being an inferior teacher. In teaching to the test, one focuses on a narrow scope of student demonstration, drilling standards to make students successful in a limited window of learning. There is an absence of rigor.

The problem with teaching to the test is that you cannot do it for an assessment that asks for application of knowledge. You can only teach to a test that requires rote knowledge. It is impossible to coach students to apply knowledge. Applying knowledge requires the student to have a working knowledge of the learning standard. The high-stakes summative assessments our students take are rigorous, multistep, application assessments, make no doubt about it.

Teaching to a level of rigor, on the other hand, first entails understanding where students need to be with a standard. To accomplish this, the teacher must have knowledge of both the standard and to what degree, or depth, the students are responsible for it. A teacher's job should be making sure students can demonstrate mastery at a predetermined appropriate level of rigor. This requires the teacher to understand the many ways content knowledge can be demonstrated so that students can successfully demonstrate their knowledge of a learning standard in a variety of ways.

Teachers, in order to accomplish this aspect, must have the end-in-mind approach when assessing their standards. This mind-set requires teachers to start with the summative and work backward from there, identifying where students need to be prior to introducing the content. This process forces teachers to analyze their learning standards and the vocabulary required of the standard and identify modes in which the students may be required to demonstrate their knowledge.

Teachers using this approach are not only able to assess the rigor of what students will need to be ready for but also important information in terms of the vocabulary that is associated with the learning standard, both academic and nonacademic. Teachers can also analyze the different ways of assessing the learning standard outside of traditional means, possibly accompanying them with graphs, charts, or graphic organizers that sometimes slip kids up.

The pitfall here is that, many times, educators are consumed with the "right now" and material coverage versus material depth. One cannot determine depth without seeing where we need to lead the students. This pitfall leads us to rely more on introducing learning objectives, assuming students will take on the rigor through osmosis. We cannot allow our teachers to get caught up in coverage, as surface coverage of the curriculum leaves our students no better off than when they first came to us.

Just think: You do not just head out for vacation without knowing the destination. You identify where you are going; then you decide how you are going to get there. The glaring difference between teaching to the test and teaching to a level of rigor is that one is focused on a narrow scope of questioning and the other is focused on students being able to successfully apply their knowledge to any setting.

The point of this chapter is to impart the necessity of formative assessment. Principals must have a concrete understanding of both the implementation of the practice and the use of the data formative assessment provides. In understanding both aspects, the principal must also know how each aspect applies to both teacher and student. One of the intended big takeaways of formative assessment is how it is not only a student assessment but also, equally important, a teacher assessment.

SUMMARY

Formative assessment may be the most important instructional practice a teacher can implement in his classroom. This single practice can guide instruction, evaluate student learning, and gauge teacher effectiveness. This one practice can accomplish all this and do so without a single shred of paper or without having students pick up a pencil. As much as formative assessment allows teachers to accomplish, the absence of formative assessment inhibits instruction so critically that teachers force themselves to teach against a stacked deck.

THREE POINTS TO REMEMBER

1. Know what your endgame is.
2. Match your rigor.
3. Don't be a slave to the calendar; allow formative assessment to be your guide.

Chapter Four

Are You Making Time to Get into Classrooms or Excuses That Keep You Out?

I think it is fair to say that we work harder and perform better when we know someone is watching. That is built into most people's DNA. The funny thing is, following this line of thinking, we are not much different from the kids in our classrooms. As soon as our kids think we are not paying attention, the negative behaviors come out. Same with teachers, except instead of bad behaviors, we see bad instructional practices. When we do not monitor our teachers, we essentially encourage the development of poor instructional practices.

We know this is true of ourselves but don't always apply this knowledge to our campuses. Not only do principals knowingly not apply this fundamental understanding to their campuses, but they also make excuses for not being in classrooms. There are so many false idols in the business of school administration, discipline management, budget management, meetings, and a host of other duties that keep us away from what is truly important: instruction. As principals, simply put, we need to quit making excuses that keep us out of classrooms if we are going to be serious about instruction and student achievement.

One of the most productive practices I can recommend, one that is essential to real instructional change, is carving out time to *inspect* what you expect...*frequently*.

The kicker is, most teachers would rather choose to be waterboarded than receive frequent walk-throughs by their principal. When principals conduct any kind of observation, they can see the nervousness on the faces of their teachers, so much so that it sometimes affects the teacher's classroom demeanor. So how, then, as administrators, do you walk the line of observing teachers enough to provide quality feedback to increase instructional quality while not driving teachers straight to retirement due to the stress of your being in their classrooms all the time?

To use observations as an effective tool, it is important to understand that they are essentially formal or informal. Formal observations are those used to evaluate teachers. Formal observations usually follow strict parameters and fall in line with the district's appraisal system. Formal observations happen far less often and have a smaller proactive impact on teacher instruction. Formal observations are essentially evaluative and reactive in nature.

Informal observations are used for teacher growth. They are to be used more frequently than formal observations and deal with teachers as a coach would a player during practice. Players understand that, through practice, they get better at their sport. During practice, players expect to be critiqued by their coaches. They expect to make and learn from mistakes in this environment. This is how we would like to teachers to view our informal observations.

To further illustrate, think of formal and informal teacher observation in the same terms as formative and summative assessment. Formal observation would be the summative assessment, an evaluation of the overall product. Viewing informal observations as formative assessments, you are measuring the process and progress toward a goal. This mind-set communicates informal observations to teachers as feedback opportunities to grow as an instructor, as they relate to their use of formative assessment in their classroom with their students.

As I work through these two different types of observation, discussing their application and importance, let's begin with informal observations. These informal observations are the backbone of a principal's observation culture. This type of observation is not only conducted more frequently, but it will also be the roadmap that leads to the formal evaluation. This will be the method instructional leaders use to improve instruction on their campuses.

Remember the discussion of the principal as change agent in chapter 1? Well, for most campuses, creating the type of observation culture I describe is going to be a major change. Jumping into the practice of frequent informal observations on a campus is not going to be something welcomed with open arms, so do not be surprised when receiving some kickback from teachers.

On the ground floor of this initiative, the instructional leader must be prepared to combat the general gnashing of teeth by teachers by opening the lines of communication. Before this change becomes comfortable, the groundwork must be laid to explain the purpose and intended benefits frequent informal observation provides teachers and students. Creating an observation culture in which teachers view frequent feedback as welcomed and encouraged takes time to establish.

Initially, especially when establishing frequent walk-throughs as a new initiative, a principal can expect an immediate increase in practices deemed fundamental on the campus from teachers of all levels. This is naturally because teachers, like most people in any job, want to do what is expected of them. Teachers, knowing that at any time an administrator may be in their room looking for specific instructional practices, are going to make sure those practices are implemented at the highest level they can produce.

Another early benefit, one that comes naturally with the constant practice of these instructional practices, is that teachers increase their effectiveness in them. Understand that principals are not going to see every step along the way as teachers work on the established fundamental practices, but through effective feedback, the time between visits will allow teachers to continue to work toward mastery of the instructional practice. This elevates both teacher effectiveness and efficiency throughout the year and also increases student achievement.

In the early steps of establishing frequent informal observations as campus practice, it is imperative that teachers understand that principals are not trying to catch them doing something wrong. Principals need to work hard to convey that they are truly working with teachers to increase the quality of instruction in their classrooms.

This is important because, if teachers don't know that principals are on their side in this growth process, instructional leaders can run into situations where these observations drive a wedge between the administrative team and the staff. Teachers need to be reassured that frequent informal observation is a necessary piece in the instructional growth process.

The best part for the teacher is that this feedback is their own. Coaching-visit feedback does not need a response or require an intimidating meeting with the principal, just an opportunity to reflect on instruction. In giving your feedback, simple handwritten notes, email, or verbal communication transfers ownership of the feedback to the teacher, as there are no worries that the feedback will be used against them in future evaluations.

I discuss the importance of trust in the first chapter, and this is another area where it will be needed. The key to building trust, as discussed earlier, is understanding that trust is developed and earned, not simply gained through a position or title. Teachers will only trust a principal when they see that she is truly standing by what she says. Teachers have to see the principal in their room as the instructional leader more than as the supervisor. Granted, principals are supervisors by the nature of the position, but supervisors do not impact instruction through informal observations; instructional leaders do.

If every time a principal goes into a classroom they ding teachers for everything they are not doing and focus on everything they see them doing wrong, then tension and anxiety skyrocket for the teacher. Teachers will make more mistakes trying not to make mistakes rather than give you an accurate picture of their instructional capabilities. When conducting coaching visits, we need to make sure we are promoting an environment where teachers feel they are part of the process, not the focus of the practice.

In building a healthy observation culture, one aspect that is often overlooked is how the instructional leader can lower tension from the observation by evaluating how it is conducted. As discussed earlier, there can be a great deal of negative feelings surrounding observations. By keeping it simple, principals can naturally smooth the process. Accomplishing this can be done rather easily through reviewing the observation logistics on the campus.

To establish informal observations in the most nonthreatening way, a small measure of effort that goes a long way with teachers merely involves semantics. By referring to observations as "coaching visits" as opposed to "evaluations" or even "walk-throughs," principals can eliminate some of the negative connotations associated with their visits. Let's remove some of the stigmas and just call them what they are.

This small change totally alters the mind-set for teachers. The instructional leader shifts the practice more toward a growth mind-set than a judgmental mind-set. By altering the language we use to refer to these observations, we also alter the perception of our intentions. A growth approach can be perceived in a much more positive light than a judgmental approach. The ultimate goal is to knock down as many perceived barriers as possible on the front end of establishing the observation culture for a campus.

Another way to lower the intimidation factor for your teachers is by eliminating as many of the formalities of these visits as we can. Traditionally, walk-throughs are scheduled and logged and often have time requirements. It is understood that many appraisal systems require a certain number of visits: Some are timed, but as discussed earlier, treat those as separate entities. Observations with those characteristics would fall into the formal-observation category.

When referring to coaching visits with your staff, try as much as possible to avoid these logistical constraints. Coaching visits do not necessarily need to be tracked, and they definitely do not require time constraints. Logistical constraints of feedback scream formality. Remember: keep it simple, with email, notes, and even hallway conversation. Working to keep these informal coaching visits informal will go a long way with your teachers. Keeping this process as informal as possible communicates to the teachers that this is a process that you are both working together toward.

In continuing to discuss feedback logistics, we must take a hard look at what we traditionally allow to drive our feedback practices. The first place to look is the forms we use. Sadly, forms drive the feedback we provide teachers. Oftentimes, administrators get locked into the forms required from our appraisal systems. Other times, we simply get wrapped up in looking more toward what is easy for ourselves and not taking into account how we make practices look to our staff.

When administrators are allowed freedom to deviate from formal appraisal-system forms, they traditionally choose to expedite the walk-though process. Administrators want something to make their lives easier. It is difficult to choose a form that requires more of the evaluator in a position where time is limited and where principals are constantly pulled away to other tasks perceived to be of higher importance. Making a small concession in this area may translate into a more welcoming view of observation by teachers, and that should be the goal. The more comfortable teachers are in receiving feedback, the more receptive they will be in changing.

After reviewing the logistics of how feedback is provided, it is now important to discuss the actual act of giving feedback. Always keep in the mind that possibly the most important key to creating a healthy observation culture is the teachers being able to count on the principal for quality feedback. As important as quality feedback is, there are right and wrong ways to present it to teachers.

As with the forms we use to provide feedback, something to think about when actually giving feedback is providing opportunities for open response. Providing for open response allows positive interactions between the teacher and administrator in this one visit. First, it personalizes the process, providing an authentic feel from the principal to the teacher. Once again, the administrator is working to smooth the process.

Second, and more importantly, it provides an actionable, detailed means to address a situation. Open response forces the principal to paint the picture, both of what is being seen and what the expectation is. When allowing for this aspect of feedback, the instructional leader helps eliminate gray areas between teachers and principals. Providing open-response opportunities naturally encourages dialogue and facilitates the communication necessary to influence instructional growth and change.

Another important aspect to consider is to not create a system that requires someone to look for everything under the sun. Remember that these are coaching visits, usually brief in nature. If the administrator can hone in on one to three instructional practices and has the ability to document what he sees, he will be better able to produce richer detail that will help the teacher use the information. Having to check for twelve items is just that: checking to see if a practice is being attempted.

The benefit for the teacher in receiving detailed feedback on one to three instructional practices versus seeing how many out of ten instructional practices they attempted is the difference between night and day. One comes across as authentic and student driven, while the other seems almost lazy and completely administrator driven, a slave to time. It also sends a much stronger message to the teacher about how the principal values instruction.

As with messages sent to teachers, one message is sent from a manager, while the other is clearly from an instructional leader. It does not take a highly trained educator to see the difference in effort between the two. When only being checked for practices implemented, teachers receive no information on their degree of effectiveness. In reality, checking the box does not even really communicate positive or negative implementation of an instructional practice, just that it was observed, good or bad.

In discussing how instructional leaders provide quality feedback, some parameters should be noted. The feedback that principals provide needs to be actionable and tied to stated, specific expectations. Teachers need to be able to do something with the feedback, to incorporate it into their classroom. If principals want a teacher to continue a practice, she needs to know exactly what they observed and how that was an example of good practice. Feedback from the principal needs to provide the teacher with the ability to replicate what was observed as quality instruction.

Another important aspect of quality feedback is specificity. Specificity in feedback avoids generalities and provides a way for the instructional leader to pinpoint aspects of instruction to discuss with a teacher to impact instructional change instead of attempting a blanket change. Feedback should simply state observations, positive or constructive, and it generally asks a question for the teacher to reflect on.

Principals need to avoid simply stating "Good job" or "Really enjoyed your lesson today!" Feedback of this nature is essentially a waste of time for both parties, administrator and teacher. Unless the principal can follow up on what was "good" about specific instructional strategies or what instructional strategies he "enjoyed," he wastes people's time. To make the mistake of writing feedback to increase good feelings or morale is a detriment to the teachers and therefore to the students in the building. This is why specificity is so important.

Principals cannot forget that it is just as important to be specific about poor instructional practices as it is about good practices. Sometimes principals fall into the trap of thinking they are done by calling out the poor practice. For example, a principal might write feedback similar to "I would like to see more questions and student interaction." Okay, that could be true, but what is the teacher going to do with that? A better approach may be as follows: "Hey, I enjoyed the opportunity I had today to watch part of your lesson. One thing I think would really take your kids to the next level would be if you were to increase the number of questions you asked to check their understanding. For instance, you could have identified someone to ask what the motives for colonization were that you have been discussing in class. That would lead directly to identifying another student to explain what specifically Spain's motives were. One last thing, make sure you have a specific idea of what you want to hear in their responses. I am looking forward to stopping by again soon. If you have any questions, please let me know."

This feedback accomplishes much of what I have discussed to this point. The instructional leader specifies exactly what he views the issue to be, increasing questioning. He also identifies why the practice would benefit the teacher's instruction, checking for understanding. Finally, he provides actionable feedback by suggesting ways to accomplish what was being asked of the teacher.

Another poor feedback practice is getting caught up in checking the boxes. This practice is kind of a mixed bag of all the negative feedback practices I have discussed to this point. Whether the lesson was good or bad, teachers are left with nothing actionable with checked boxes. Think of what teachers are left to digest with a form with half the boxes checked while the others are left blank. How can instructional leaders expect feedback of this nature to impact instructional practices in any way? The answer is really simple: they cannot.

When the "good job" feedback is delivered to create good feelings or improve morale, go ahead and see what kind of opposite effect will come from it. The teacher will feel as if she did something wrong without a way to fix it or will view the principal's feedback as meaningless. The latter carries the added effect of eroding the principal's credibility among the staff.

Another characteristic of quality feedback practices is in not mixing your responsibilities. This can happen as administrators feel the time crunch and try to accomplish killing two birds with one stone. Coaching visits are instructional in nature. Remember the goal is to grow teachers instructionally. This is not necessarily the place to reprimand noninstructional issues and dilute the overall purpose of this specific visit.

For example, a principal would not want to address a teacher's tardiness or her missing a meeting along with his feedback on her classroom instruction. That is not to say to avoid addressing those issues; they just need to be addressed in another setting. Trying to merge tasks in this way may reflect negatively on the observation culture a principal is trying to establish.

One might think the key to unlocking the maximized value of informal-observations feedback stops here. The thought is that if administrators can create rich feedback on a handful of specific instructional strategies, instruction and student achievement will skyrocket across campuses. It is not necessarily that easy. Earlier principals were asked to make more of the limited time they already had in order to get into classrooms more. Well, there is more to being effective in this practice, and once again, the lack of time principals have will not be an acceptable excuse.

The next key to walk-through feedback that drives instructional improvement is follow-through. This step may be more important than writing the feedback itself, both in practicality and teacher morale. This is true because, if instructional leaders simply provide the feedback and never check to see if instruction is improving, they have essentially wasted their own time and the teacher's. Then, in addition to wasting time, the administrator has diminished the value of the process by sending the message that instructional growth is merely a suggestion as opposed to a requirement.

A lack of follow-through by the instructional leader can lead to a campus culture problem. When the principal does not follow through on instructional feedback, he essentially conditions teachers to believe they can choose whether to incorporate the instructional leader's feedback into their instruction. Coaching visits and the feedback are part of a growth process, but the expectation is not that the feedback is a suggestion. The instructional leader conveys this message through follow-through to ensure that the feedback is being implemented.

Over time, the ultimate goal of frequent observations is the discussions that are borne from these visits between instructional leader and teacher. These conversations center on the fundamental practices the principal is looking for in classrooms. Administrators begin the transition from being the gatekeeper of knowledge about these practices to witnessing individual teachers, through these conversations and feedback, begin to take ownership of these instructional practices.

Teachers, through this ownership, will start looking for and finding the freedom to tailor these practices to their teaching styles and begin to make them increasingly more effective than anything the principal could have planned for going into the process. When the campus gets to this point, teachers will begin inviting administrators to come into their classrooms to provide feedback on their tweaks and adjustments. At this stage, instruction begins to hit levels of effectiveness that have no bounds moving forward.

Principals will have developed a culture of instructional innovation based on practices deemed essential to student learning while at the same time allowing teachers the freedom to sculpt and mold these into instructional practices that increase student achievement. Mind you, they may still prefer principals not to come so much, but the culture being fostered is worth the necessary uneasiness.

In transitioning from the formative version of observations (informal coaching observations) to the summative version (formal observations), administrators will need to change both their approach and mind-set. In informal coaching observations, principals work with the success of the teacher in mind. In formal observations, they are giving a final exam. Principals must take this opportunity to evaluate teacher effectiveness and be able to make determinations based on whether the needs of students are being met and students are successful.

The formal teacher observation is entirely student driven, as we are looking at whether the teacher in the classroom is the best possible option for the students. When conducting these observations, the mind-set shifts to looking at how students relate to the instruction provided by the teacher. This is where instructional leaders determine if instructional practices are leading to student learning or not.

For many, this is the most difficult leadership role as principal. This is where principals are charged with making the tough decisions on staff. Principals have to decide if a teacher is growing at an acceptable pace or needs to move on. In the cases where teachers need to move on to benefit students, principals as instructional leaders need to have the intestinal fortitude to move in that direction.

The difficulty in this process is the human factor: knowing the person being evaluated and having an attachment to the people we lead, as all leaders do. At the end of the day, instructional leaders need to remember that we are in a kid business and not an adult business. We have to ultimately make decisions that are best for the students who walk through the doors of our campuses each day, not the adults.

That is not to say that principals should stop having relationships and attachments to their teachers, as that is impossible, but they must be able to do what is best for students regardless of those relationships and attachments. Too often, principals enjoy the fun parts of being in administration, the kids, the staff, the activities, but forget that there are tough moments in leadership. Often it is the tough moments that define leaders, and this is just as true in schools. It is important to realize that it is your ultimate responsibility as the instructional leader to ensure that you have the best possible teachers for every student.

There are several factors to consider when evaluating teachers: the teachers' way of relating to students and their ability to build relationships, their content knowledge, and their instructional prowess, to name a few. Also, as instructional leaders, when evaluating teachers, we have a responsibility to take into account where they are in their growth. As discussed in chapter 1, teachers are at different development levels as they spend more time in the profession. How they conduct their classes often reflects this and should be taken into account.

Sometimes we get lucky, as many teachers will make life easy for the principal because either they are simply amazing or they do not want to follow your lead and choose to find greener pastures elsewhere. However, the teachers who do not make life easy place the principal in the position of making the decision for them. It is in these decisions that instructional leaders, those who look out for the kids in the classrooms, make themselves invaluable to a campus.

In making these decisions, the instructional leader must determine whether a teacher can be successful in helping students achieve at acceptable levels. This does not mean the teacher has to have met their peak, as in many situations teachers may still be on the upswing in their careers. In other cases, teachers may be at their peak, and their peak may not be good enough. It is often a fine line but one the principal is charged with making.

You could also have teachers on the downswing of their careers, who do not necessarily want to put forth the effort to be successful anymore. These teachers can present a unique challenge because they may also be well-revered teachers due to longevity on the campus. Regardless of the situation, it is the role of the principal to understand where the teacher is on the spectrum and have the intestinal fortitude to make the correct decision for kids.

If you identify teachers who are growing, the decision with this group is whether they are growing at an acceptable pace or whether there is just too much growth needed. The goal of every instructional leader is to grow their teachers. This is especially true for those new to the profession; if we do not make efforts to grow the rookies, our profession will eventually fail. It is important to grow our profession, but the principal's decision has to be about kids first.

As for the teacher who is growing, normally principals are looking at a teacher relatively new to the profession. These teachers usually have a probationary period that principals can operate within. If a principal is not positive that this group will be effective classroom teachers by the end of their probationary periods, usually two to three years, he should recommend that they move on. If, after two to three years on the campus, they have not shown enough growth to gain the principal's full confidence, additional time is not going to change that, and the students are ultimately the ones to suffer.

Also, principals must deal with complacent teachers. If they cannot be brought out of that mind-set, it may be time for them to leave. Principals have to have teachers who want to constantly improve at their craft. Students change every year, and we have to be able to adjust to them. If you cannot adapt, you die. In teaching, the inability to adapt loses kids. If a kid loses a year of instruction, it takes two years to gain it back. It is the principal's responsibility as an instructional leader to ensure that negligence does not take place on campus.

Finally, principals may have teachers whom they inherited but who do not have the ability to be successful classroom teachers. This scenario is the result of incompetent leadership. For whatever reason, decisions were made that did not reflect the needs of students but the needs of adults. As stated in the previous paragraph, allowing ineffective teachers to work in classrooms is instructional negligence, and students on campus pay the price.

It is in these variable situations that the principal cannot be afraid of the growth-plan option or teacher-in-need-of-assistance (TINA) plan. Too often, this option is associated with pink slips. This could not be further from the truth. If created and implemented correctly, a growth plan could be exactly the life raft that a teacher needs to turn both instruction and their careers around.

When implemented successfully, the teacher and principal discuss the instructional concerns together, both with equal input, and work to put a plan in place for growth. Both parties discuss what the outcome needs to be and the route to success. To be successful, the principal should set incremental checkpoints to measure progress toward the goal, with opportunities to discuss feedback toward the progress. As tasks are completed and coaching visits occur, the goal is for the teacher to increase effectiveness and efficiency.

However, everyone needs to know when to cut bait. Some of us will never be Olympic sprinters, no matter how hard we train. It needs to be stated again that this is a kid business, not an adult business, and we have to develop teachers who are best for kids. Not everyone is cut out for this business. Just like those trying to be Olympic sprinters, not everyone gets to compete in the Olympics.

Regardless of which group a teacher may be part of, the principal wants to see the teachers' best during their formal observations, which weigh so heavily in decisions on teachers' future employment. So when principals conduct these high-stakes evaluations, how do they go about notifying teachers? Traditionally there are two trains of thought. Administrators' opinions are almost split down the middle on how much input teachers should have when scheduling these formal observations.

One school of thought is to give teachers a vague time window, usually a week, allowing administrators the ultimate control of when the observation is done. The rationale for this option is so that teachers cannot prepare the infamous "dog and pony show" that administrators on this side of the fence despise. The dog and pony show allows teachers to teach to the evaluation and not give an accurate picture of their instruction the other roughly one hundred seventy days a year.

The other train of thought, advocated in this book, is to allow teachers to schedule the day and time, thereby allowing, if not encouraging, the dog and pony show. Why in the world would someone advocate this option? Simply put, the administrator should want to see, without any excuses, the best possible lesson teachers can put together when they hold all the cards. If the principal is doing her job of being in classrooms as frequently as discussed, there really should not be any surprises. Principals should know what they are getting.

Taking this option to the next level even involves having a conference with the teacher prior to the observation to outline what it is the principal will be looking for and providing the teacher the opportunity to clarify any expectations or ask any questions. This practice is very similar to what we are asking from the teachers in their classrooms with the end-in-mind mind-set with their students. Lay all the cards out on the table, and take away any excuses through a process of transparency.

For the same reason, we advocate for the end-in-mind design in our classrooms to prepare our students for success on their summative assessment; the same is true of the teacher during observations. No one hires teachers with the intention of firing them. Principals want all teachers growing in their craft. So why would we not lay out all our cards and see if teachers can meet our expectations? It seems only fair with so much on the line, both for the teacher and essentially their students.

Now, with the structure in place, delineating between formal observations and informal coaching visits, it is important to identify and discuss the areas in which principals need to get out on their our own in order to make this practice successful. Over many generations, we have created perceptions among teachers to cement their beliefs that observations are bad things. In order to rectify these notions, we have to not only know what they are but also where they come from.

As noted at the beginning of the chapter, people are going to work and try harder when they know someone is watching. It should not be a stretch to expect each teacher on a campus to get a coaching visit weekly. Once again, do not expect teachers to feel warm and fuzzy about the prospect of having an administrator in their rooms four times each month over the course of a nine-month school year. Go in knowing they will have reservations about seeing administration that often.

The lack of that warm, fuzzy feeling is self-inflicted, however, due to the doctrine administrators have created. Principals have over time conveyed observations in two ways, sometimes incorporating both at the same time. First, principals have devalued observations as formality. This message is sent when we treat observations as something done once a year, something that principals basically check the box on. In taking part in this practice, principals communicate observations as a task instead of what they should be, that is, an opportunity for professional growth.

The second is that we fail to see that perception matters. Almost as important as what we say is how we say it. A lesson for all principals to learn and understand is that perception is reality, and it drives the culture on a campus. We have trained our staffs that "good" teachers do not need as many observations as "bad" teachers. We have accomplished this perception a couple different ways.

The first is due to the age-old belief that observations are part of the process to gain "documentation" on teachers whom principals do not want on campus. This is very similar to what I discussed with growth plans. This negative view severely hinders our attempts to have teachers view principals in their classrooms as a positive. This creates an enormous self-imposed dilemma for administrators.

We are trying to create a culture of observation as a form of providing feedback to make every teacher better, yet through our self-imposed perception issue, teachers perceive increased walk-throughs as a negative reflection of their overall performance. Basically, every time an administrator comes into a classroom, teachers are thinking, "Oh great, they are back. What did I do now?"

Another way we add to the misperception of observations is by sending mixed messages. As principals, you must be mindful that you cannot make morale decisions that devalue the practice. One of the biggest mistakes principals make is letting better teachers off the hook. Principals need to make sure that the same rules and expectations apply to everyone equally.

As discussed earlier, teachers for the most part are perpetually nervous about administrator observations. Sometimes, as a good-faith gesture in an attempt to ease teacher anxiety, principals tell them in some form or fashion that their observation is a formality, nothing for them to worry about. In an attempt to be supportive, principals take away teachers' main opportunity to grow; we devalue the observation practice for them.

Another way principals perpetuate this perception is in what they choose to let slide by or in the assumptions they make to defend teachers doing what does not necessarily sit well with them. Principals do this when they see teachers they like practicing poor instructional strategies and allow them to continue without correction. These small gestures speak loudly to teachers and establish the observation culture and expectations negatively. This tells teachers that principal observations are only important for the few and not everyone. As with any initiative, setting the proper tone and expectations can be the difference between success and failure.

A quality instructional leader wants every teacher moving forward; they want every teacher to grow. In this situation, principals act like the parent who gives their child everything they want, has no rules, and wonders why they get walked all over when they were just trying to be their friend. As the principal, your role as an instructional leader is not necessarily to be your teachers' friend. You always want to support your staff, but your responsibility is to take every opportunity possible to ensure that your teachers are honing their craft so that the students in the building are getting the best possible instruction every day.

The best thing a principal can do for the stronger teachers is to create an environment that communicates that they are not immune from criticism. As the proverb goes, iron sharpens iron. The principal should be just as present in the strongest teacher's class as they are in the weakest teacher's class. It is an easy job to provide feedback for the weaker teachers. Their instructional practices are not as strong, and there will be refinements that are easy to see and many times even blatant mistakes to address. The challenge is providing feedback that improves already-strong instruction. The principal needs to be the iron that sharpens the best teacher on campus.

Up to now in this book, the focus has been mainly on the principal's role with teachers, but regarding teacher observations and teacher feedback, the principal's role in dealing with assistant principals is also important. A disconnect between the principal and her assistant principal in this area can create a major problem for the instructional leader in her attempts at building a healthy observation culture.

It is incredibly important that, prior to attempting to create any sort of observation culture, the principal must clearly outline and define the roles and responsibilities for the administrators they work with on campus. Every topic covered up to this point needs to be filtered down to your assistant administrators. As the instructional leader, you must discuss how feedback should be provided, what common language should be used in feedback, and how often they are expected to be in classrooms.

Another important aspect about observations, whether formal or informal, is to have regular conversations with your administrative staff concerning the strengths and weaknesses of the staff. It would not be unreasonable to expect to have regular, weekly meetings. Just as we want regular evaluation of our students' progress, the same should be required for teachers by administration.

These regular meetings should resemble meetings we may have for students in intervention programs. Principals will first need to discuss, as an administrative staff, what they feel each teacher's area of growth is while identifying the interventions to help that teacher to move forward. Then, just as we do with students, the administration staff would meet to discuss whether the strategies are working to help the teacher grow. If it is determined that the strategies are not successful, you would, as a group, decide what the next steps are.

The final piece to share with your administrative staff is imparting a sense of priority to the observation plan. As the instructional leader, the principal must be able to convey how essential the observation plan is to the instructional success of your staff. It must be communicated that, when everything is going south, observations are the priority. The principal must expect that, when prioritizing tasks during the day, when some tasks get bumped, observations should never fall into the "bumped" category. In fact, any other item should get bumped to ensure that regular observations are conducted.

The ultimate goal is to ensure that the administrators are all on the same page throughout the process from classroom to classroom. Each member of the group conducting observations is going to use the same language and have the same expectations, the same understanding of what the campus's fundamental practices look like when they are implemented, and the same agenda for each teacher. Most importantly, your staff will always hear the same message. This is pivotal because getting feedback from multiple people not saying the same thing increases frustration levels with the staff at a rate you cannot combat.

The positive result of this is that administrators get to see teachers practicing their craft. Teachers, just like athletes, musicians, or other professionals people are often awed by, get better with practice. One of the biggest failures of our profession is always talking about instructional change at the beginning of the year before the kids arrive, and then, by November, our initiatives lose steam because we never come back to them. The initiative loses importance among the staff because it is no longer examined and therefore is assumed to not be expected. It becomes another initiative gone with the wind.

As noted earlier, everyone does their best when they believe someone is watching. If people are going to find ways to cut corners, they are going to find that opportunity when no one is watching. Principals, make sure you find time to be in classrooms. It is not just for the "gotcha" moments, for there is no way to evaluate instruction without knowing what is going on. There is no way to have a teacher take you seriously in an instructional conversation if they know you are only in their room every so often when you get the time. We show what we prioritize by what we spend our most valuable commodity, time, on.

The fundamental takeaway is that the responsibility for poor instructional habits is shared by teachers and administrators. It is easy to see what is important to people by taking a look at what they spend their time doing. If administrators do not spend time in classrooms observing and giving feedback on instruction, teachers do not see instructional practices as a priority on campus. If teachers perceive that the principal does not deem instruction important, why would they see a need to hone that craft?

SUMMARY

In order to accomplish everything in this book, principals have to quit making excuses that keep them out of classrooms and begin finding ways to get more time in classrooms. In order to fulfill the requirements of an instructional leader, the principal has to get out of the office. It is well understood the number of tasks a principal is responsible for in a limited amount of time each school day, but people will see what is important to a person by what he spends his time on. The one task we cannot ever shirk is that of being in classrooms evaluating instruction. So many of the tasks that may cut into this responsibility can be done at other times, but this is the one responsibility that can only be done when teachers and students are together. Principals cannot shortchange this one and expect to maximize student achievement.

THREE POINTS TO REMEMBER

1. Have the right priorities.
2. Know which priorities you are communicating to your teachers.
3. Quality feedback is the lifeblood to teacher growth.

Chapter Five

Become a Data Storyteller

This chapter is placed at the end with a purpose. The information in this chapter may very well be the most important for principals and instructional leaders. Up to this point, the book has established principals' importance in hiring, growing, and dismissing teachers; it has discussed their role as instructional leaders, as well as the importance of formative assessment and of finding time to get into classrooms. All of those aspects of a principal's job are null and void if they cannot interpret the data they have gained.

As discussed earlier, the only way to evaluate the instructional program is through data. Not only do you need data, but you also have to know what to look for in the data. An issue arises when the teachers do not have a leader competent in sifting through the data. Know this as fact: If there is not an instructional leader to help interpret the data correctly, the risk is that it will be used incorrectly, and the overall instructional plan suffers. An instructional plan can only successfully be evaluated through the proper interpretations of formative and summative data.

The situation we have to guard against is settling for a Cliff's Notes approach to campus data. Too often principals have an infatuation with the simplicity of pass or fail when looking at assessment data. Whether a student passes or fails is merely the title of the story. There is much more information the assessment data tells us about our students. Being able to break down and understand this data in its entirety makes everyone's job easier.

Principals who succumb to this Cliff's Notes approach to campus data run the risk of falling prey to two potential pitfalls. First, skimming over data can lead to the principal making misinformed decisions. Principals making decisions without a real understanding of the data can result in undercutting teachers, devaluing the instructional program, and eroding trust from their staff. This happens when principals shoot from the hip on decisions involving classroom instruction, curriculum, or general practice with an interpretation of the data that may provide false information due to its limited scope.

When discussing how misinformed decisions are made, people immediately look through a negative lens. Yes, skimming over data can lead principals to believe they are in a worse position than they actually are, but there is a flip side to that coin. Skimming data can also give the principal a false sense of confidence, resulting in tables turning in the end. The same limited scope of understanding can also paint a false positive outlook. This outlook is just as dangerous, if not more, due to nothing being addressed because everything seems to be hunky-dory.

Under the surface, there is another foundational data principle. Instructional leaders need to be keenly aware that the data often tells just as much about the instruction as it does the learning. In order to be an effective principal in this domain, one must understand all that the data is telling and, more importantly, be able to communicate to teachers everything it is saying about classroom instruction. Remember: data is the ultimate evaluator of the instruction provided on our campuses.

Prior to having these conversations with teachers, the staff must be assessed in their knowledge and understanding of data. Teachers can be the biggest offenders of Cliff's Notes data. As mentioned in previous chapters, teachers are notorious for judging their ability based on test scores. As the instructional leader, it is the principal's responsibility to train the staff on the intricacies of their data so they can fully understand what the numbers are telling them, both about their instruction and the students' learning.

Before instructional leaders train teachers, though, they themselves need to be confident in using data and know what to look for in it. They need to know how to sift through learning objectives. Principals need to be able to evaluate the difference between a student guessing on an answer or guessing on the distractor. Can the principal decipher how to use data to drive scope and sequence? The principal should be able to determine the difference between knowledge of a standard versus being unfamiliar with a question format. These things and more are discussed in this chapter.

Before the principal can even begin discussing the data, the data the campus is using must be credible. When determining the credibility of data, the instructional leader should start at the data source. Prior to digging into any data, the principal must evaluate the exams producing the data. The principal as the instructional leader has a responsibility to ensure local exams replicate the rigor and question types students can expect on high-stakes summative exams that will gauge their overall academic achievement.

In determining the credibility of your data through the source, locally created summative assessments, imitation is the sincerest form of flattery. Who is responsible for creating these assessments for your campus? Are these people familiar with the expectations? In making all attempts to replicate the summative high-stakes assessment your students will ultimately be judged against, those creating the assessment must be well versed in what those assessments look like, as well as have an understanding of their rationale. At the same time, principals must ensure that teachers are teaching at the level they are assessing.

As the instructional leader, principals must study and evaluate question types and the ancillary material, such as text and dialogue boxes and the varied graphic organizers students will need to navigate on these assessments. Making sure that instruction reflects the use of this information throughout the year on local summative assessments ensures that your data can reliably predict student success. It also ensures that students are able to demonstrate their knowledge in varied settings.

One of the other hurdles confronting principals in upholding data credibility can be teachers. Inherently, campuses are going to have teachers on different levels of ability to know and interpret their data. Data-competent teachers can drill down and unlock the story the data is telling. They look for gaps in instruction and areas for student and self-growth. These teachers are using data to impact classroom instruction.

Some teachers may not be as competent, those discussed earlier who judge themselves based on passing percentages. The teachers in this group may reveal to a principal an underground practice referred to in this book as "test stacking." Test stacking is something the instructional leader needs to be aware of to ensure viable data. The practice of test stacking can severely inhibit the instructional leader's ability to evaluate an instructional program.

Stacking test data is the practice of teachers creating assessments, typically at a minimal rigor, that will make them feel good about their instructional efforts due to their students' high scores. This practice works well for the teacher in the short term but can lead to a harsh reality check for principals in standardized exams that evaluate student achievement and essentially campus effectiveness. False data of this nature is the type that gets principals fired when scores come back significantly lower than what was forecast all year on local summative assessments.

Combating this scenario is not difficult. To ensure good data, the principal must have an end design in mind and be able to impart it to their teachers. When creating assessments, both formative and summative, everyone needs to have a concrete understanding of the level of rigor and the varied ways students may need to demonstrate their learning of the standard. Once teachers have that understanding, they must drive their instruction to meet those levels.

The difficulty comes if this is a paradigm shift. In many cases, this may be a major paradigm shift. In these situations, change is hard, and results are not immediate. In fact, results may significantly dip before they increase. This dip is the result of students adapting to a level of rigor that is not familiar to them. This is where the trust built between the principal and the teacher is imperative. Teachers need to feel supported and know that they will have help with the shift in philosophy.

The trust piece is important because, as stated earlier, especially in places where this is new practice, scores may dip significantly at times, shaking some teachers' confidence, evoking a sense of insecurity with their standing with the principal. This is due to the adjustment period for increasing rigor in the classroom. Both students and teachers feel this adjustment period. Both sides will struggle initially as they rise to meet the new standards through varied instructional practices and increased student expectations. As the instructional leader, be prepared to identify and remedy the instructional deficiencies that are resulting in your data dips.

What a principal gains in having credible data is confidence in his ability to diagnose weaknesses. No two teachers are the same, and our data story allows us the opportunity to respect that fact. Our data story allows the instructional leader to essentially create individualized instructional plans for teachers similar to those we do for students. It also allows the instructional leader to identify positive instructional practices that we can share with other teachers within content areas. This allows principals to perpetuate good instruction and work on instruction that can improve.

Another point to emphasize with teachers is that, when they push rigor and expectations, students do not always follow along on the time schedule. When the data is not what teachers and principals would hope for, the knowledge gained can be incredibly powerful for the instructional plan. Teaching students where they are, correcting misunderstandings, clarifying the muddy waters—that is what teachers do. Knowing the data helps us know where to start.

For example, this chapter discusses assessment data, both formative and summative, that may come back with low results. Some people may see failure or an opportunity to pass blame, but in owning the data, one can find powerful information even in low results. An instructional leader or teacher may be able to identify holes in prior knowledge, gaps in instruction, or simple disconnects that are easily fixed with students. It all depends on how hard we want to look to determine the why.

When instructional leaders try to interpret data, it is important that they identify the various levels of data and understand how deep the data actually goes toward providing principals a roadmap to student achievement. Table 5.1 provides several data sets. The information in each is contrived but allows us an opportunity for a more in-depth conversation on how to approach data.

This data set would be considered surface-level data. This data provides a general overview of an assessment. It simply shows the number of students tested, their average score, and the number of students meeting the standard. It also divides the students into demographic populations. The purpose of showing this data set is to show that principals all too often make decisions based on surface-level data, and this information really does not give much insight at all to student learning. In fact, this data arguably provides nothing that can impact student achievement or instruction.

This data set provides about the same information as if you missed an entire football game and all you had to know how the game went was the scoreboard. You can tell who won and lost. What you do not see is whether the game was closer than the final score shows or was it not as close as you would believe. Were there a couple of really poor individual performances that severely impacted the overall outcome of the game? Finally, the score-

Table 5.1. Data Sets

	Total Students	Percent Score	Percent Meeting Standard
Anywhere JH	129	68.35	73.42
Econ Disadvantage	57	64.24	71.93
Sub-Pop 1	53	67.85	79.28
Sub-Pop 2	24	62.56	73.46

board does not speak to which team was the most prepared. Just looking at the scoreboard seems to create more questions than answers.

For so many years, administrators have trained teachers that this is the end-all-be-all data set for determining student effectiveness. This is an issue principals have to answer for as instructional leaders, as we are responsible for perpetuating this poor data practice. Administrators have reverted to the bottom line for years. Principals have routinely chosen to set a minimum standard for whole-group achievement, as opposed to looking at data to impact every child. Principals have done this while also lacking the initiative to find the reasons behind student achievement, whether good or bad, to either replicate or improve instructional practices.

Within this data set, a couple numbers are heavily referenced but of little value. The first number is the percent score. The average percent score from a group of students provides absolutely no instructional value, yet it is a number routinely used to determine how well a class or group of students did on an assessment. Educators will make decisions on staff and curriculum and a vast number of other decisions based on this percentage, which does not tell us anything about learning objectives, student responses, or where students actually struggled with the content.

For example, a principal is looking at the following data set with student summative exam scores of 100, 90, 90, 60, 60, and 50 percent. The average of those six scores is 75 percent. If the principal were to look at only the 75 percent average score, she might feel secure with it initially, as 75 percent may be perceived as an acceptable score. What the principal would miss is the reality that half of the students in the data set did not meet standard.

The second number to be careful with is the percent meeting standard. This number carries considerably more value than the percent score but is still quite superficial. This number does provide information on how students performed on a group of learning standards but is one of those title-of-the-story numbers. The mistake is when judgments are made based solely on this number. This number represents a group of learning standards, but we still have not identified which standards within the group were ones students struggled with. We are also still left without any information pertaining to individual student achievement.

How this number may mislead a principal can be seen in the data set in table 5.1. In referencing the 73.42 percent of students at Anywhere Junior High, a principal may perceive it as an acceptable score. The exam is testing four learning goals; the two scenarios that follow speak very differently to the 73.42 percent meeting standard.

In Scenario 1 (table 5.2), there is not much variance between student achievement data among learning goals. This information allows the principal to determine that students have an even understanding of the learning goals assessed. In Scenario 2, however, the instructional leader can see that students were not successful on learning goals 3 and 4, and he can begin to tailor the next steps in remediation to increase student achievement. Principals who do not push further into their data will have failed to see the issues presented in Scenario 2.

Placing too much value on either of these surface-level data sets may lead one to believe they are in either a better or worse situation than they are. Either false outcome leads to the instructional leader making ill-informed decisions. Being able to correctly interpret this data may prevent the instructional leader from making decisions that can negatively impact instruction.

The ill-informed decisions I refer to are generally about not being able to know whether the testing group is close to a much higher mastery level or how the testing group can be in much greater need of remediation than these surface numbers show. Ill-informed decisions of this nature lead to a poor foundation for any instructional program because teachers don't know whom to help or how to help them.

The data set in table 5.3, however, dives deeper and provides the principal real information to impact instruction and thereby the ability to increase student achievement. This set provides several pieces of information: from gauging success toward specific learning objectives and question type to

Table 5.2. Scenarios 1 and 2

Scenario 1	
Learning Goal 1	76%
Learning Goal 2	70%
Learning Goal 3	74%
Learning Goal 4	73%
Scenario 2	
Learning Goal 1	98%
Learning Goal 2	88%
Learning Goal 3	52%
Learning Goal 4	55%

answer-choice rationale. This information, when deciphered correctly, can be used to shape lessons, guide tutorials, and focus questioning practices. However, as with any data set, not understanding what the data is telling you can lead to misfires and misguided decision making.

One key to learning the most from this data set is to understand that each category, column, or row does not necessarily stand alone but usually works in conjunction with the others to tell the story we are looking for. For instance, in comparing learning goals 2.4 and 3.3, someone could conclude that the students performed significantly better on learning standard 3.3, when in reality a strong case could be made for the opposite. Similarly, one could argue that the students struggled mightily on learning goal 5.6, but a piece of the data there tells a different story. This piece of data is about the ability to differentiate between a guess and a distractor.

To truly see all there is to see in this data set, some focus points must be defined. First, when looking into an item analysis, the principal as an instructional leader must be able to look at answer choices and differentiate between those that were a "guess" and those where students were confused by a "distractor." Being able to tell this part of the story allows the teacher to determine if students are missing a question due to a lack of understanding content or an inability to apply their learning to a certain question/answer format. The instruction required to right the ship is much different in each scenario.

Consider the difference in responses to question 4 and question 11. If the principal were to simply look at the percentage of students choosing the correct answer for each question, she would be disappointed that only 48 percent got question 4 correct, and only 61 percent got question 11 correct. A

Table 5.3. In-Depth Data Set

Learning Goal	Learning Goal (%)	Question Number	A (%)	B (%)	C (%)	D (%)	Answer
1.3	80	2	80	7	8	5	A
2.4	68	5	8	2	3	87	D
2.4	68	4	48	17	15	20	A
3.3	80	7	0	3	92	5	C
3.3	80	1	2	75	3	20	B
3.3	80	9	9	72	11	8	B
5.6	61	11	4	32	61	3	C

deeper look tells us a much different story, though. In question 4, the answer choices are basically spread evenly. This is what we would term a *guess*. This answer spread should alert you that students were not strong on the content, as they could not find the answer in any of the choices.

Question 11 shows a much different situation. Only 61 percent of the students were able to choose the correct answer, but 32 percent locked into one of the other answer choices. This is *choosing the distractor*. The distractor is that answer choice the test makers so kindly throw in there to trick our students. *Distractors* refer to answer choices with the sole purpose of distracting students from the correct answer.

Typically, when choosing answers, students can eliminate two choices as not likely, leaving them to choose between the remaining two, one of which is obviously the correct answer, but the other is the distractor. The distractor is intentionally included to draw the attention of students as a possible answer choice. For the students to choose the correct answer, they usually need to be able to determine, through their knowledge of the content, why the distractor is incorrect. The following is a tangible example: Consider Bill, who delivers newspapers each morning. Table 5.4 shows how many papers he delivers each day. What is the average number of papers he delivers on a weekday?

a. 51.3
b. 48.7
c. 46
d. 49

In this example, the correct answer is D. The average number of papers delivered on weekdays, Monday through Friday, is forty-nine. The answer choice B is the distractor in this set. This has two traits of a distractor: it is closest in value to the correct answer, and it is the average of all seven days, a choice a student may make in haste.

Instances where the students choose the distractor over the correct answer at such a high percentage, in this case 93 percent, can be seen as a positive because educators can determine that it is not necessarily a content issue but

Table 5.4. Number of Papers Delivered Each Day

Sunday	Monday	Tuesday	Wednesday	Thursday	Friday	Saturday
47	52	49	50	46	48	49

more likely an outside-factor issue. When looking for outside factors, usually you are going to look for question types, vocabulary, or unfamiliarity with graphics. If we are able to identify and remedy the issues leading students to choose the distractor, student achievement increases significantly.

Another reason principals can view distractor issues as a positive is that they are easy to rectify. These solutions require introducing students to the nonacademic vocabulary that trips them up or finding the graphic in the question that students did not understand. As the instructional leader, this requires relying on your teachers to have that end in mind to foresee as many of the obstacles as possible. This often requires content expertise, and as mentioned earlier, the principal cannot always be the content expert. These are usually the fixes that get the big light bulbs to go to on when teachers are going over mistakes with the class.

Another gem for the instructional leader is the learning goal percentage. This data can easily be misinterpreted, leading to false information. This data is often misinterpreted, like other data, due to reliance on the number as our sole point of reference. In table 5.3, look at learning goal 2.4 at 68 percent. Just looking at the number, one would think that that learning goal was not taught adequately. Once again, looking deeper can determine that there is an outside-factor issue.

Learning goal 2.4 was assessed twice on this assessment. In this situation, it is important to look at the student responses for each question before making overall impressions of student mastery of the learning goal. On one question, 87 percent of the students were correct. This percentage would be considered a success. On the other question used to assess learning goal 2.4, only 48 percent of the students answered correctly.

Looking further into this question can determine that it had a "guess" (as defined earlier) response, due to the evenly distributed responses over the other choices. This tells the principal that the students have knowledge of the learning goal but were unable to apply that knowledge to this specific question for some reason. The principal's next steps here would be to open a dialogue with the teacher to examine the question and determine what threw the students off.

At this point, it is important for the principal as the instructional leader to see that there is a very clear instructional blueprint provided to increase student achievement through careful review of an item analysis data set similar to table 5.3. The principal can see and relay a data-driven plan for each question for either small-group or whole-class remediation. The plan is specific and actionable because, if data is deciphered correctly, educators can determine exactly why students went astray.

This data set can also be used as a powerful tool for teachers to evaluate their own instructional practices. Using this data properly clearly informs the teacher if the instruction provided was effective or if reteaching is needed to ensure mastery of the learning goal. It also provides the teacher information about whether students are getting ample opportunities in the classroom to apply their learning in the various assessment settings.

As I continue to dig deeper into our data, there is another layer to look at in order to get a clearer picture of exactly what plan is needed to further increase instructional efficiency and student achievement.

The table 5.5 data set presents individual student scores. In a real scenario, a principal would obviously see data from a much greater number of students. Even with the small data set, the intended point can be made. First, let's look at the typical pitfall for principals. The mistake they make with this data set is in simply identifying the students who did or did not meet standard. The seven students who did not meet standard have different stories among them but more in common with the three students who met standard than one would think.

Let us begin by looking at the students who did not meet standard. If the principal were to look at these students as a group, the remediation plan would lack effectiveness. The students on any assessment can be divided, at a minimum, into two tiers, if not more, based on each student's raw-score

Table 5.5. Data Set with Individual Student Scores

Student	Raw Score	Percent Score	Met Standard
Student A	3	49	No
Student B	4	52	No
Student C	7	61	No
Student D	7	61	No
Student E	8	64	No
Student F	9	67	No
Student G	9	67	No
Student H	10	70	Yes
Student I	11	73	Yes
Student J	12	76	Yes

distance from the standard. Once principals become comfortable with the data, they will be able to see natural breaks that establish student groups.

In this small mock data set, the group could easily be divided into a tier of students two to three questions away from the standard and a second tier four or more away from the standard. This not only provides smaller groups for remediation but also allows the teacher to tailor these sessions based on student need. Teachers are able to meet the needs of the students rather than wasting instructional time with larger groups of students with a much more varied remediation need.

Viewing the group of students who did not meet standard in this way, a teacher is more able to move these students toward the standard through a more appropriate remediation plan than a one-size-fits-all model geared simply toward students not meeting standard as a whole. Conducting tutorials and remediation to a group of students who only missed standard by one to three questions should look vastly different from tutorials or remediation to a group of students who missed meeting standard by a significant number of questions.

To apply this practice, let's look at what each group's remediation may look like. Remediation for a group of students on the cusp of meeting standard may resemble a conversation between the students and teacher. The students may spend the majority of the time explaining their need for clarification on the finer details of the content. The group that is furthest from standard may need reteaching. The key point here is to teach the material in a new way. We do not want to fall into the trap of teaching it the same way, expecting different results. I believe there may be a term for that.

There are still two groups that routinely get left out of additional instruction because they met standard. One of those two groups met standard by only one to three questions. These students are in just as much danger of not meeting standard as the tier of students who barely missed. As easy as it is to celebrate improvement by reaching the kids who were close to standard, neglecting the students on the other side of the fence can quickly come back to bite you. Simply looking at the data to see who passed and failed will leave these students behind every time.

Possibly the most neglected group (when looking at any piece of data but especially the data set in table 5.5) is the group of are the students who did not meet the high-level standard. Just as we look to those who did not meet standard, it is important to address the students who we expect to achieve at our masters or commended level. These students are often afterthoughts because educators know they will pass, but they fail to measure if they are growing and moving forward in the content year to year. Teachers need to ensure that all students show growth, and there is no other way to do so than through looking at the data.

In mentioning student growth, how do we go about measuring if students are growing? Before I can answer that question, I need to define our expectations for student growth and discern its importance to campus teachers. For our purposes, *growth* is ensuring students are moving forward in their content knowledge year to year. It is an easy assumption that, after a full school year in a classroom, students should have gained measurable knowledge.

The worst possible scenario with student growth is if students pass their required summative assessments each year, but no one notices that every year they pass by a smaller margin, eventually resulting in their, surprisingly, failing summative assessments. The entire time they fell through the cracks and never received the remediation that could have been provided to avoid the entire situation. This is a situation that sadly happens all too frequently, as these are the students who typically "surprise" us by failing end-of-year high-stakes accountability exams.

How sad is it that students can go an entire year in a classroom and not show any academic growth? So how do we identify these students? These are locally based questions that each learning organization must answer. Regardless of the decisions made, there needs to be a data measure to ensure that students are moving forward and, if not, that they are provided the proper interventions to get them moving again. Measuring and monitoring growth for all students, not just the lower-level students, is a practice we cannot afford to let slip through the cracks.

To identify students who are struggling in the content is important but not the sole job of the data we gather. Let us now turn our attention to how data tells a story about our instruction. Data provides information on both student struggles and teacher struggles. It is important for an instructional leader to look at both and know how to adjust both the teacher and student sides accordingly. As discussed throughout this book, data evaluates instruction. The student side is obviously dealing with remediation and reteaching, but what is to be gained from the teacher side?

Working through the tables in this chapter, you have seen how data is used to establish tutorial groups, to identify questions that zero in on learning goals, and to disassemble answer choices to identify instructional needs. All this information takes the guesswork out for teachers in identifying where students struggle and how to reach them to close gaps in their learning. Without the data, teachers would be grasping for straws about where to begin with students who are not meeting expectations.

Moving forward, the ultimate job of a data storyteller is to pass the torch to the rest of her staff. At some point, for the campus to really grow in using meaningful data to impact student learning, the teachers need to learn how to tell the stories. The goal is almost the same as a pyramid-scheme salesman's. At the beginning it's just you, but over time you get a couple of people under you, and then they get a couple under them, and so on.

A further illustration is similar to the Bible proverb of how giving someone a fish will feed him for a day, but you teach him to fish and you feed him for a lifetime. If the principal is constantly feeding and interpreting the data for the teachers, they never truly own the data, and a powerful tool in instructional reflection loses its value on a campus. Teachers owning their data fosters a new level of instructional growth in their classrooms.

The best principals reach the ultimate goal of training their teachers to look at data in the same light and to tell the story themselves. If principals can get teachers to use data to avoid or limit the number of students struggling the same way the next time the content is taught, teachers maximize student achievement and instructional efficiency. Each time a summative assessment is given, administrators and teachers have a tool to evaluate lessons, curriculum, and scope and sequence.

As with any other initiative, it will take time for teachers to get comfortable with it, and there is definitely a process to go through. If the principal goes into a building and just throws the teachers to the wolves with expectations that quality data analysis will be done after one in-service or one after-school faculty meeting, he is setting himself and his staff up to fail miserably. A well-developed plan of action is a necessity. In putting a plan together, understand that you will need to prepare for differences among your staff. You are sure to have teachers who are much more comfortable than others in this process.

Based on many factors beyond your control, every teacher's willingness or comfort will vary. Your job as the instructional leader will be to decide what is needed to ensure each teacher's success in this endeavor. Also understand that each teacher, just like the kids in his classroom, is going to learn this process at a different rate. Patience is the key, as their getting to where the principal wants them is essential to unlocking their greatest potential as instructors in the classroom.

In the initial stages, it will be important to spend a significant amount of time with the staff, moving through the different levels and explaining expectations and what to look for at each level. Remember: for many teachers this is going to be very unfamiliar and in some cases will seem almost like learning a new language. In addition to working through the data, principals are sure to run into unexpected issues, such as teachers who do not appreciate technology. The majority of your data reports will be acquired through some sort of data system. Work through these small obstacles and keep the focus on the big picture.

Showing the staff how to get the most out of their data will be similar to moving through a lesson cycle. In the beginning, there will be a great deal of introduction. The principal will discuss ideas the teachers are not familiar with in many cases. The key in this phase is patience. As discussed earlier, the principal will have teachers at different levels of knowledge of data practices. Principals need to use those who are very comfortable to their advantage and have them guide the more reluctant teachers through the process. This is also a great way to build leadership capacity within the staff.

This initial phase will, for the most part, be administrator led. This stage will likely be whole group and will be the principal's opportunity to open the staff's eyes to the wonderful world of data. The key at this stage is to remember that it is all introductory at this point; to expect the staff to leave the training and go out into the world as data experts is setting up failure. Make sure to communicate this to the staff. Explain to them that there will be bumps in the road, and everyone will make it through in the end.

Principals will then move into a period of guided practice. During this period, the principal will be working with the teachers, sifting through their data individually. It will almost resemble a shoulder-to-shoulder model as data comes in for each teacher. There will be a lot of coaching involved, as the principal will walk teachers through in a one-on-one approach. As discussed in earlier chapters, principals are going to need to provide different levels of assistance with different levels of teacher experience and be mindful of the traits of novice, experienced, and veteran teachers.

As principals move forward into this guided-practice stage, one of the hardest aspects to understand is that, as instructional leaders, principals are going to have to relinquish some control over the data. They are going to have to get comfortable with letting teachers take the data, make it their own, and inevitably make mistakes. The power is in the struggle, however, and through the mistakes the teachers will make, instructional leaders will have the opportunity to have rich discussions about data. As an instructional leader, this should be a point of excitement.

Finally, principals eventually achieve the goal of the teachers coming to them with their data and being able to tell their own stories. This step essentially marks the independent-practice portion of the journey. At this point, the teachers are coming with their data and working through the data sets; they are able to give the principal a plan of action. It is at this stage that the principal has accomplished something. When the staff gets to this stage, principals have unlocked instructional powers that can overcome issues others would view as insurmountable.

When reaching this ultimate goal, principals have empowered their teachers to become their own data storytellers. At this point, the principal has become a facilitator and takes a role of guiding the conversation. During this stage of the process, the principal's responsibility shifts from telling the teachers what their data says to asking probing questions to get the teachers to tell what their data says. In having these instructional conversations, the principal has unlocked an instructional power that unleashes the instructional capacity of the staff exponentially.

Once principals are able to grow the staff to where they are able to tell their own data stories, principals open the floodgates to greater instructional change. At this time, principals no longer have to be the sole instructional leader on campus responsible for all innovation and change. What they begin to foster now are conversations on what teachers believe are the next steps for campus instruction. Just as principals asked teachers to step out of their comfort zones when implementing the instructional plan, principals now need to step out of *their* comfort zones and be willing to loosen the reigns and begin sharing ownership of the instructional plan.

As teachers become more adept in their understanding of their data, they will be increasingly able to assess their own practices, as well as those on campus. This should not be seen as a negative but as an extreme positive. Remember how I discussed the importance of teaching styles? When principals grow teachers to the level where they self-reflect on their practices and understand how they can better integrate that style to the campus's core beliefs, principals have achieved a masterful victory for instruction on their campus.

SUMMARY

Each campus's data tells its own unique story. Many people use campus data to assess surface information, such as who passed and who failed. A principal who is an instructional leader understands that who passed and who failed is simply the title of the story. Instructional leaders understand how to use data to find the "why" and know how data can be used to create a plan of action to address student and teacher needs. To do this, principals need to become familiar with the different layers of data and how each layer works in coordination with the others to tell a much larger story.

THREE POINTS TO REMEMBER

1. Do not settle for the Cliff's Notes version of your data.
2. Listen to what the data is saying and react.
3. Do not be the data gatekeeper.

About the Author

Josh Martin, EdD, has been a Texas educator for seventeen years. In that time, he has been a teacher, coach, assistant principal, principal, and director of special education. He is currently the chief academics officer at Farmersville Independent School District. In all of these roles, he has been driven to work for the best in kids. In his current position, working for the best in kids comes from mentoring teachers and campus administrators to provide the best learning environments possible for the students in his district.

www.ingramcontent.com/pod-product-compliance
Lightning Source LLC
Chambersburg PA
CBHW030146240426
43672CB00005B/298